Introduction

Welcome to *New Maths Frameworking*!

New Maths Frameworking Year 8 Practice Book 1 has hundreds of levelled questions to help you practise Maths at Levels 4-5. The questions correspond to topics covered in Year 8 Pupil Book 1 giving you lots of extra practice.

These are the key features:

- **Colour-coded National Curriculum levels** for all the questions show you what level you are working at so you can easily track your progress and see how to get to the next level.

- **Functional Maths** is all about how people use Maths in everyday life. Look out for the Functional Maths icon  which shows you when you are practising your Functional Maths skills.

Contents

Collins

Year 8, Practice Book 1

NEW MATHS FRAMEWORKING

Matches the revised KS3 Framework

Kevin Evans, Keith Gordon, Trevor Senior, Brian Speed

William Collins' dream of knowledge for all began with the publication of his first book in 1819. A self-educated mill worker, he not only enriched millions of lives, but also founded a flourishing publishing house. Today, staying true to this spirit, Collins books are packed with inspiration, innovation and practical expertise. They place you at the centre of a world of possibility and give you exactly what you need to explore it.

Collins. Freedom to teach.

Published by Collins
An imprint of HarperCollins*Publishers*
77–85 Fulham Palace Road
Hammersmith
London
W6 8JB

Browse the complete Collins catalogue at
www.collinseducation.com

10 9 8 7 6 5 4

ISBN 978-0-00-726798-9

Keith Gordon, Kevin Evans, Brian Speed and Trevor Senior assert their moral rights to be identified as the authors of this work.

British Library Cataloguing in Publication Data
A Catalogue record for this publication is available from the British Library.

Commissioned by Melanie Hoffman and Katie Sergeant
Project management by Priya Govindan
Covers management by Laura Deacon
Edited by Karen Westall
Proofread by Marie Taylor
Design and typesetting by Newgen Imaging
Design concept by Jordan Publishing Design
Covers by Oculus Design and Communications
Illustrations by Tony Wilkins and Newgen Imaging
Printed and bound by Printing Express, Hong Kong
Production by Simon Moore

Every effort has been made to trace copyright holders and to obtain their permission for the use of copyright material. The authors and publishers will gladly receive any information enabling them to rectify any error or omission in subsequent editions.

Mixed Sources
Product group from well-managed forests and other controlled sources
www.fsc.org Cert no. SW-COC-1806
© 1996 Forest Stewardship Council

FSC is a non-profit international organisation established to promote the responsible management of the world's forests. Products carrying the FSC label are independently certified to assure consumers that they come from forests that are managed to meet the social, economic and ecological needs of present and future generations.

Find out more about HarperCollins and the environment at
www.harpercollins.co.uk/green

Practice

1A Negative numbers

1 Work out the answer to each of these.

a −5 + 8   **b** 2 − 7   **c** −4 − 9

d 2 − 6 − 3   **e** −5 + 6 − 4   **f** −3 + 8 − 2

2 Work out the answer to each of these.

a 5 − +7   **b** −7 + −3   **c** 4 − −6

d −3 − +4   **e** −5 − −4   **f** − +7 − 4 + 6

g 2 − −5 − −8   **h** −4 + −6 − +3

3 Find the missing numbers to make these true.

a −5 + ☐ = −3   **b** ☐ − 3 = −7

c ☐ − −3 = 0   **d** −2 − ☐ = 6

4 Calculate these.

a 5 − 9   **b** 2 − 6 + 3   **c** −2 +−5

d 9 − −7   **e** −3 − +5 − 4

5

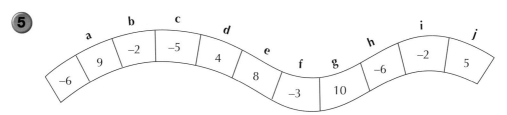

  i Add each number to the number on its left. Write down your answers. For example, **a** 9 + − 6 = ?

  ii Subtract each number from the number on its left. Write down your answers. For example, **a** −6 − 9 = ?

6 Calculate these.

a 5 × −3   **b** −8 × −5   **c** −3 × 10

d −2 × −2   **e** 14 × −3   **f** −4 × −2 × 5

g 2 × −3 × −1   **h** −10 × 6 × −10

7 Calculate these.

a 16 ÷ −2   **b** −6 ÷ −6   **c** −9 ÷ 3

d 12 ÷ −3   **e** −100 ÷ 10   **f** 20 ÷ −2 ÷ −5

g −36 ÷ −3 ÷ −4   **h** 40 ÷ −5 ÷ −2

8 Copy and complete these chains of calculations.

a

(−2) —+3— ( ) —−5— ( ) —−2— ( ) —+1— ( )

b

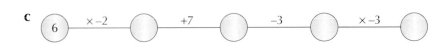

(−1) —×4— ( ) —×−2— ( ) —−3— ( ) —+5— ( )

c

(6) —×−2— ( ) —+7— ( ) —−3— ( ) —×−3— ( )

d

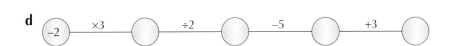

(−2) —×3— ( ) —÷2— ( ) —−5— ( ) —+3— ( )

Practice

1B HCF and LCM

1 **a** Write the first 10 multiples of these numbers.
  i 3   **ii** 6
  iii 10   **iv** 12
 b Use your answers to **a** to find the LCM of these pairs of numbers.
  i 3 and 6   **ii** 6 and 12
  iii 6 and 10   **iv** 10 and 12

2 **a** Write out all the factors of these numbers.
  i 12   **ii** 18
  iii 20   **iv** 30
 b Use your answers to **a** to find the HCF of these pairs of numbers.
  i 12 and 18   **ii** 12 and 20
  iii 20 and 30   **iv** 18 and 20

3 Find the LCM of these pairs of numbers.
 [**Hint:** Write out the first few multiples of each number.]

  a 4 and 8   **b** 6 and 10
  c 7 and 8   **d** 9 and 12

4 Find the HCF of these pairs of numbers.
 [**Hint:** Write the factors of each number.]

  a 14 and 35   **b** 8 and 20
  c 12 and 30   **d** 15 and 24

Practice

1C Square numbers and square roots

5

1 Write down the values of the following. Do not use a calculator.

a $\sqrt{64}$ **b** $\sqrt{1}$ **c** $\sqrt{121}$
d $\sqrt{81}$ **e** $\sqrt{0}$

2 Calculate these. Do not use a calculator.

a $\sqrt{9} \times \sqrt{16}$ **b** $\sqrt{81} \times \sqrt{4}$
c $\sqrt{100} \div \sqrt{25}$ **d** $\sqrt{9} \times \sqrt{16} \div \sqrt{36}$

3 With the aid of a calculator, write down the value of these square roots.

a $\sqrt{196}$ **b** $\sqrt{784}$ **c** $\sqrt{8281}$
d $\sqrt{344\,569}$ **e** $\sqrt{33\,640\,000}$

4 Make an estimate of these square roots, then use the calculator to see if you were right.

a $\sqrt{169}$ **b** $\sqrt{484}$ **c** $\sqrt{900}$
d $\sqrt{3600}$ **e** $\sqrt{2209}$

5 Use your calculator to work out these square roots. Round your answers to the nearest whole number.

a $\sqrt{200}$ **b** $\sqrt{13}$
c $\sqrt{732}$ **d** $\sqrt{8000}$

6 Sometimes, the difference between two square numbers is another square number. For example, $10^2 - 8^2 = 100 - 64 = 36$, which is a square number. Use the numbers in the cloud to find more of these.
Write each answer like this: $10^2 - 8^2 = 6^2$.

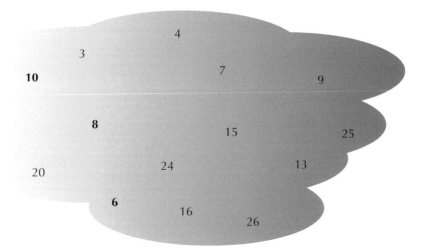

7 a Copy and continue this pattern to make eight rows. Work out all of the answers.

1   =
1 + 3   =
1 + 3 + 5   =
1 + 3 + 5 + ... =

b What can you say about the answers?

1D Prime factors

1 Calculate these products of prime factors.

a $2 \times 5 \times 5$ **b** $2 \times 2 \times 2 \times 3$ **c** $2 \times 3 \times 7 \times 7$

2 Use a prime factor tree to write each of these numbers as a product of its prime factors.

a 6   **b** 18   **c** 32
d 70   **e** 36

3 Use a prime factor tree to write each of these numbers as a product of its prime factors. Start your diagram with the numbers in brackets.

a 100 (4×25) **b** 128 (8×16) **c** 180 (10×18)
d 135 (9×15) **e** 132 (6×22) **f** 210 (10×21)

1E Sequences 1

1 Follow the instructions to generate sequences.

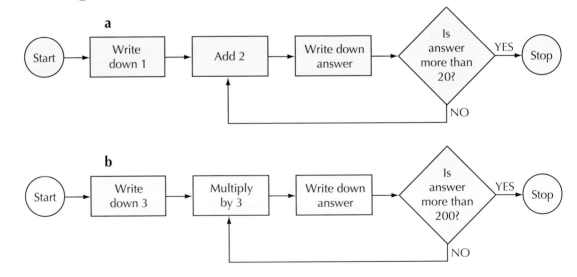

2 **a** Find the term-to-term rule for each of these sequences.

    i 5, 8, 11, 14, 17 …

    ii 30, 28, 26, 24 …

    iii 2, 10, 50, 250 …

  b Find the next two terms in each sequence.

3 Given the first term and the term-to-term rule, write down the first five terms of each of these sequences.

  a First term 8, rule: add 4   **b** First term 50, rule: subtract 5

  c First term 3, rule: multiply by 4   **d** First term 64, rule: divide by 2

4 These patterns of dots generate sequences of numbers.

a

4   7   10   13

b

2   5   9   14

  i For each sequence, draw the next two patterns of dots.

  ii Write down the next four numbers in each sequence.

Practice

1F Sequences 2

1 You are given the first term and the term-to-term rule. Write down the first five terms of each sequence.

  a First term 2, term-to-term-rule: multiply by 5

  b First term 3, term-to-term-rule: multiply by 2 then add 4

  c First term 5, term-to-term-rule: subtract 1, then multiply by 2

2 Copy and complete the table for each sequence.

  a Rule: multiply term position number by 3.

Term position number, n	1	2	3	4	5
Term		6			

  b Rule: multiply term position number by 4 then subtract 1.

Term position number, n	1	2	3	4	5
Term		7			

3 The *n*th term of each sequence is given below.

a $3n - 1$ **b** $2n + 5$ **c** $5n - 3$ **d** $10n + 10$

Copy and complete this table for each sequence.

Term position number, *n*	1	2	3	4	5
Term					

Practice

1G Solving problems

1 Paving slabs 1 metre square are used for borders around L-shaped ponds.

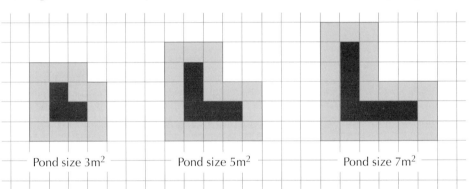

Pond size 3m²   Pond size 5m²   Pond size 7m²

a How many slabs would fit around a pond of size 9 square metres?
b Write a rule to show the number of slabs needed to make a border around L-shaped ponds.

2 Write a rule to show the number of matches needed to make these shapes.

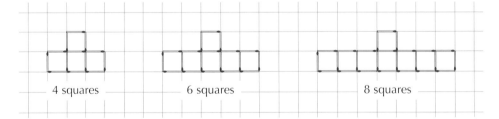

4 squares   6 squares   8 squares

CHAPTER 2 Geometry and Measures **1**

Practice

2A Parallel and perpendicular lines

1 **i** Which of these sets of lines are parallel?

a
b
c

d
e
f

ii Which of the sets of lines are perpendicular?

2 **a** Copy each of these lines on to squared paper.
On each diagram, draw two more lines that are parallel to the first line.

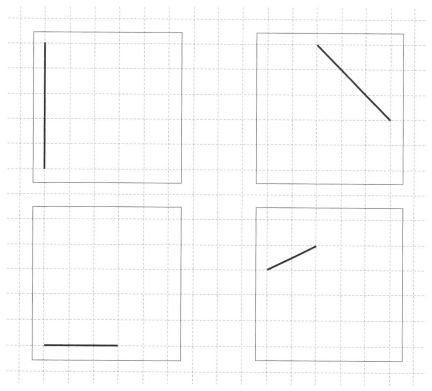

b Make another copy of each of the lines.
On each diagram, draw two more lines that are perpendicular to the first line.

3 Look at this diagram.

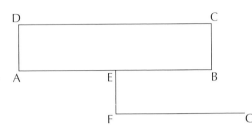

a Which lines are parallel to the line AB?
b Which lines are perpendicular to the line AB?

2B Measuring and drawing angles

1 Describe each of these angles as acute, right-angled, obtuse or reflex.

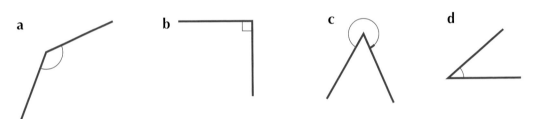

a   b   c   d

2 Measure the size of each of these angles, giving your answers correct to the nearest degree.

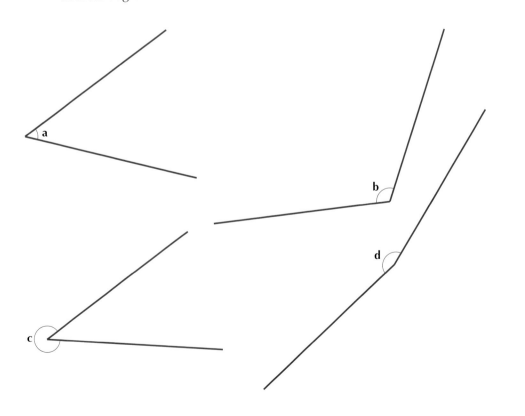

3 Draw and label these angles.

    a 70°   **b** 35°   **c** 135°

    d 200°   **e** 340°

4 Measure the four angles in quadrilateral ABCD.

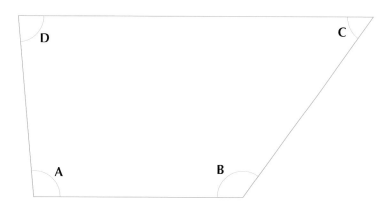

Practice

2C Calculating angles

Calculate the size of each unknown angle.

1   **a**   **b**   **c**

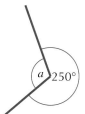   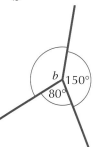   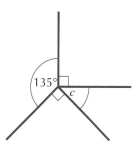

2   **a**   **b**   **c**

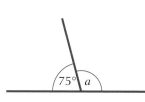   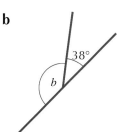   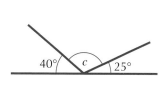

3   **a**   **b**   **c**

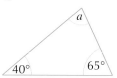   

5

1 Copy this table and, in each column, write the names of all possible quadrilaterals that could fit the description.

2 pairs of equal angles	Rotational symmetry of order 4	Exactly 1 line of symmetry	Exactly 2 right angles	Exactly 4 equal sides
	Square			

[**Warning:** A quadrilateral could be in more than one column!]

2 **a** Some quadrilaterals have two pairs of equal angles. Which are they?
   b Some quadrilaterals have two pairs of equal sides. Which are they?

3 **a** A quadrilateral has exactly two equal angles.
     What type of quadrilateral could it be?
   b A quadrilateral has three equal angles.
     What type of quadrilateral could it be?

4 Some quadrilaterals have diagonals that intersect at right angles.
   Find as many as you can. Illustrate your answers with drawings.

1 Construct these triangles. (Remember: label the vertices and angles.)

a

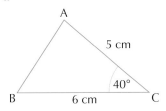

b

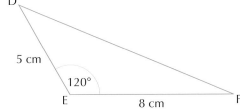

c

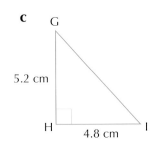

2 Construct these triangles. (Remember: label the vertices and angles.)

a

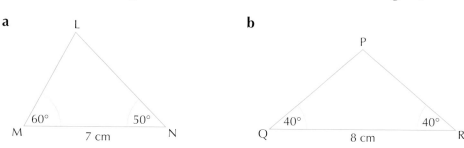

b

c

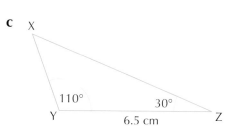

3 **a** Construct the triangle ABC, with AB = 6 cm, BC = 11.5 cm and ∠B = 35°.
   b Measure side AC, giving your answer correct to the nearest millimetre.

CHAPTER 3

Statistics **1**

3A Probability

1 Copy this probability scale.

Impossible   Unlikely   Evens   Likely   Certain

Label your scale with each of these events.
a Choosing an ace from a pack of 52 cards – there are 4 aces in a pack.
b You will experience it raining some time in the future.
c You are travelling down an unknown road. The next bend is left.
d A person can walk on water unaided.
e A wine glass breaks when you drop it onto the floor.

2 Write down an event that is:

   a unlikely   **b** certain   **c** likely   **d** impossible

3 A child is asked to choose a lucky number from one of these:

1   2   3   4   5   6   7   8   9

Which of each of these pairs of events is more likely to be chosen?
a An odd number or number less than 5
b A prime number or even number
c A multiple of 3 or multiple of 4
d A triangle number or cube number

4 Imagine these quadrilaterals are cut from plastic and placed in a bag.

rectangle   parallelogram   square   rhombus   kite   trapezium

You choose one at random.
Copy and complete these sentences by filling in the missing probability words: impossible, unlikely, evens, likely, certain.

a Picking a shape with a right angle is …
b Picking a shape with at least two equal sides is …
c Picking a shape with four angles is …
d Picking a shape with four equal angles is …
e Picking a shape with no equal sides is …
f Picking a shape with only three sides is …

Practice

3B Probability scales

1 100 rings are placed in a box. 20 are gold, 25 are silver, 16 are plastic and the rest are copper. A ring is chosen at random.
What is the probability that it is:

a gold   b silver   c plastic   d copper
e not gold   f not silver   g not plastic   h not copper?

2 This diagram shows 12 dominoes.

A domino is chosen at random. Calculate the probability that it:

a has a 5
b is a double
c has a total of 7
d is not a double
e does not have a 5
f does not have a blank
g does not have a 3

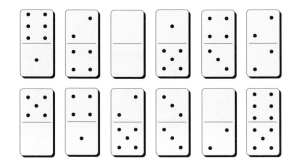

3 The probability that a large egg box contains a cracked egg is 0.12.
What is the probability that a large egg box does *not* contain a cracked egg?

4 Megan has a bag of equal-sized sweets.
5 are mints, 3 are toffees and 2 are jellies.
  a What type of sweet is Megan most likely to pick out?
  b What is the probability of Megan, picking at random:
    i a toffee   **ii** a jelly   **iii** a mint?

5 Joy has eight rabbit kittens. Three of these are male.
  a How many female rabbit kittens does Joy have?
  b What is the probability of choosing one of these kittens out, at random,
    and it being:
    i female   **ii** male?

6 Kirk has a CD in his car which had 7 vocal tracks out of 10. He selects a
track at random. What is the probability that this track in not vocal?

Practice

3C Experimental probability

1 The numbers of days it rained over different periods are recorded in
this table.

Recording period	Number of days of rain	Experimental probability
30	12	12 ÷ 30 = 0.4
60	33	
100	42	
200	90	
500	235	

  a Copy and complete the table.
  b What is the best estimate of the probability of it raining?
    Explain your answer.
  c Estimate the probability of it not raining.
  d Is there a greater chance of it raining or not raining?

2 If you drop a matchbox, it can land in one of three positions.

END   EDGE   SIDE

a Drop a matchbox 10 times. Copy this tally chart and record your results.

How matchbox landed	Tally	Frequency	Experimental probability
End			
Edge			
Side			

b Calculate the experimental probabilities.
c Repeat the experiment. This time drop the matchbox 20 times.
d Repeat the experiment with 50 trials.
e Which is the best estimate of the probability of the matchbox landing
   i on an end   **ii** on an edge   **iii** on a side?

CHAPTER 4 Number 2

Practice

4A Fractions and decimals

1 Cancel each of these fractions to its simplest form.

  a $\frac{5}{20}$ **b** $\frac{10}{12}$ **c** $\frac{21}{35}$

  d $\frac{16}{20}$ **e** $\frac{12}{18}$ **f** $\frac{30}{25}$

2 Write each of these decimals as a fraction with a denominator of 10 or 100. Then cancel the fraction to its simplest form.

  a 0.7   **b** 0.15   **c** 0.2   **d** 0.65
  e 0.8   **f** 0.24   **g** 0.06   **h** 0.64
  i 0.02   **j** 0.55

3 Convert these fractions to decimals.

a $\frac{7}{10}$　　b $\frac{13}{100}$　　c $\frac{3}{10}$　　d $\frac{1}{4}$

e $\frac{97}{100}$　　f $\frac{1}{2}$　　g $\frac{1}{10}$　　h $\frac{9}{100}$

i $\frac{17}{50}$　　j $\frac{3}{100}$

4 Convert these fractions to decimals. Change each denominator to 100 first.

a $\frac{7}{50}$　　b $\frac{9}{20}$　　c $\frac{8}{25}$

d $\frac{27}{50}$　　e $\frac{13}{20}$

Practice

4B Adding and subtracting fractions

For Questions 1–3, cancel your answers and write as mixed numbers, if
necessary.

1 a $\frac{3}{7} + \frac{2}{7}$　　b $\frac{5}{9} + \frac{1}{9}$　　c $\frac{1}{12} + \frac{5}{12}$

d $\frac{5}{8} + \frac{1}{8}$　　e $\frac{7}{8} + \frac{7}{8}$　　f $\frac{3}{10} + \frac{9}{10} + \frac{7}{10}$

2 a $\frac{4}{5} - \frac{1}{5}$　　b $\frac{8}{9} - \frac{5}{9}$　　c $\frac{7}{8} - \frac{3}{8}$

d $\frac{9}{10} - \frac{3}{10}$　　e $\frac{11}{12} - \frac{3}{12}$

3 a $\frac{4}{7} + \frac{4}{7}$　　b $\frac{7}{9} - \frac{1}{9}$　　c $\frac{3}{8} + \frac{7}{8}$

d $\frac{11}{6} - \frac{7}{6}$　　e $\frac{1}{3} + \frac{2}{3} + \frac{2}{3}$　　f $\frac{13}{15} - \frac{8}{15}$

g $\frac{5}{6} + \frac{5}{6} - \frac{1}{6}$

4 Write each of the following as a mixed number.

a $\frac{7}{4}$　　b $\frac{5}{2}$　　c $\frac{9}{6}$

d $\frac{13}{2}$　　e $\frac{11}{3}$　　f $\frac{8}{7}$

g $\frac{7}{3}$　　h $\frac{14}{5}$

Practice

4C Multiplying fractions

1 Use grids to work out:

a $\frac{1}{4}$ of 28　　b $\frac{3}{5}$ of 30

c $\frac{1}{3}$ of 36　　d $\frac{3}{4}$ of 24

2 Calculate each of these.

a $\frac{4}{9}$ of 36 kg   b $\frac{5}{6}$ of 30 ml   c $\frac{2}{7}$ of 28 cm   d $\frac{1}{4}$ of 52 km

e $\frac{3}{7}$ of 42 cm   f $\frac{7}{10}$ of 50 grams   g $\frac{3}{5}$ of £80   h $\frac{7}{8}$ of 640 litres

3 Calculate each of these. Cancel your answers and write as mixed numbers if necessary.

a $2 \times \frac{3}{8}$ b $4 \times \frac{3}{7}$ c $9 \times \frac{5}{6}$

d $7 \times \frac{2}{5}$ e $6 \times \frac{8}{9}$

4 Calculate each of these. Cancel your answers and write as mixed numbers if necessary.

a $\frac{2}{3} \times 6$ b $\frac{3}{7} \times 4$ c $\frac{4}{5} \times 7$

d $\frac{2}{9} \times 8$ e $\frac{3}{8} \times 4$

Practice

4D Fractions and percentages

Do not use a calculator. Show your working.

1 Write these fractions as percentages.
Convert each denominator to 100 first, if necessary.

a $\frac{49}{100}$ b $\frac{7}{100}$ c $\frac{21}{50}$ d $\frac{13}{25}$ e $\frac{11}{20}$

2 Work out each of the following.

a   7 as a percentage of 10   b   19 as a percentage of 25
c   13 as a percentage of 20   d   33 as a percentage of 50
e   3 as a percentage of 5   f   1 as a percentage of 20

3 Milton drinks 27 cl of a 50-cl bottle of orange.
a   What percentage did he drink?
b   What percentage remains?

4 A company employs 25 workers. At the last general election, 13 voted Labour, 10 voted Liberal Democrat and the remainder voted Conservative. Calculate the percentage vote for each party.

5 Stuart took a maths test lasting 20 minutes.
He spent 8 minutes on the Algebra section, 7 minutes on the Number section and the remaining time on the Shape and Space section.
What percentage of the time did he spend on each section?

6 16 out of 25 pupils in class 8A passed their maths test. 13 out of 20 pupils in class 8B passed the same maths test. Which class had the better results?
[**Hint:** Calculate the percentage for each class.]

4E Percentage increase and decrease

Do not use a calculator. Show your working.

1 Calculate these.

    a 20% of £80   **b** 5% of 20 kg

    c 15% of 140 cm   **d** 90% of 400 litres

2 Mrs Walker left £45 000 in her will. The money was divided between her three children as follows:

    Derek 60%
    Maria 25%
    Jason 15%

How much did each child receive?

3 Three people each withdrew a certain percentage of their bank balance from their bank account:

    John withdrew 30% of £300

    Hans withdrew 75% of £640

    Will withdrew 15% of £280

    a How much did each person withdraw?
    b Which person has the largest remaining bank balance?

4   **a** Increase $40 by 20%.   **b** Decrease 200 kg by 5%.

    c Decrease 70p by 60%.   **d** Increase 2000 m by 25%.

    e Increase 140 ml by 15%.   **f** Decrease £250 by 20%.

5 Before a typing course, Leon could type 60 words per minute. The typing course increased his speed by 15%. What was his speed after the course?

6 'Zipping' a computer file reduces its size by a certain percentage. Find the sizes of these files after zipping.

    a 500kB file reduced by 20%   **b** 740kB file reduced by 5%

    c 840kB file reduced by 25%   **d** 1900kB file reduced by 90%

7 Marvin's average score on the computer game Space Attack was 150.

    a After buying a new gamepad, his average score increased by 20%. What was his new average score?
    b Marvin went on holiday. When he returned, his average score had decreased by 15%. What was his new average score?

4F Real-life problems

 1 Dan bought a calculator from a shop for £23. The shopkeeper paid £20 for the calculator. What percentage profit did the shopkeeper make?

 2 Maria bought a skateboard for £25. She sold it two months later for £18. What was her percentage loss?

 3 An odd job man kept a record of his income and costs for each job. Copy and complete this table.

Job	Costs (£)	Income (£)	Profit (£)	Percentage profit (%)
4 Down Close	100	135		
High Birches	50	91		
27 Bowden Rd	25	42		
Church hall	20	34		

 4 Three dealers offer the following repayment options for a car with a marked price of £12 000. Which works out the cheapest overall?

Trustworthy Cars   20% deposit followed by 12 monthly payments of £900
Bargain Autos   15% deposit followed by 8 monthly payments of £1400
Future Car Sales   25% deposit followed by 6 monthly payments of £1650

 5 Amanda deposited £30 000 in her bank. The bank pays interest of 10% per annum.

a Show that Amanda had £33 000 in her bank account after one year.
b Amanda kept all of the money in her bank for another 3 years. Copy and complete this table.

Year	Amount at beginning of year (£)	Interest earned at 10% per annum	Amount at end of year (£)
1	30 000	10% of 30 000 =	33 000
2	33 000		
3			
4			

 6 Hamid weighed 50 kg before he went on a diet. After the diet, he weighed 46 kg. What was his percentage loss in weight?

CHAPTER 5 Algebra 2

Practice

5A Algebraic shorthand

1 Write each of these expressions using algebraic shorthand.

   a $x \div 5$ **b** $3 \times b$ **c** $m \div n$
   d $p \times 3$ **e** $y \div 4$

2 Copy and complete each of these.

   a $8 + 3 = 3 + \boxed{}$ **b** $\boxed{} \times 2 = 2 \times 6$ **c** $a + b = b + \boxed{}$
   d $4 \times s = s \times \boxed{}$ **e** $\boxed{} \times h = ht$ **f** $8r = r \times \boxed{}$
   g $pq = \boxed{} \times q$

3 Solve each of these equations.

   a $x + 7 = 10$ **b** $x - 3 = 6$ **c** $x + 1 = 15$
   d $x - 8 = 8$ **e** $x - 10 = 20$ **f** $x + 13 = 40$

4 Find the expressions that are equal. Write them as an equation, e.g. $4 + s = s + 4$.

   a $5y, y + 5, y \times 5$ **b** $5 + p, 5p, p - 5, p + 5$
   c $a - b, ab, a + b, a \times b$ **d** $\frac{3}{h}, h \div 3, \frac{h}{3}$

5 Simplify each of these.

   a $4 \times 2 \times s$ **b** $5 \times 3d$ **c** $t \times 2 \times 3$
   d $5m \times 5$ **e** $a \times 2 \times 2$

Practice

5B Powers

1 Write these expressions as powers (using index form).

   a $4 \times 4 \times 4$ **b** $3 \times 3 \times 3 \times 3 \times 3 \times 3$ **c** $10 \times 10 \times 10 \times 10 \times 10$

2 Calculate these powers.

   a 2^4 **b** 3^3 **c** 2^7 **d** 4^3 **e** 10^4

3 Write these expressions as powers (using index form).

   a $a \times a \times a$ **b** $g \times g \times g \times g \times g \times g$
   c $S \times S \times S \times S \times S \times S \times S \times S \times S \times S \times S$ **d** $K \times K$

4 Simplify these expressions.

a $9 \times k \times k$ **b** $4 \times a \times a \times a$ **c** $5s \times s \times s \times s$
d $u \times u \times u \times 3$ **e** $4 \times 5 \times t \times t \times t$ **f** $r \times 4r$
g $3m \times 2m$ **h** $5w \times w \times 2w$ **i** $2j \times 2j \times 2j$

5 Write these expressions as briefly as possible.

a $m + m + m + m + m + m + m + m$ **b** $t \times t \times t \times t \times t$

6 Explain the difference between $6w$ and w^6. Write out each in full.
$6w =$
$w^6 =$

5C Like terms and simplification

1 Simplify these expressions.

a $f + f$ **b** $i + i + i + i$
c $H + H + H$ **d** $m + m + m + m + m + m$
e $u + u + u + u + u + u + u + u + u + u + u + u$

2 Write out these in full, e.g. $3t = t + t + t$.

a $4d$ **b** $6a$ **c** $8G$

3 Simplify these expressions.

a $4i + 7i$ **b** $7r + 2r$ **c** $3u + u$
d $7t - 3t$ **e** $4n - 3n$ **f** $15t - 10t$

4 Simplify these expressions.

a $3h + 2h + 4h$ **b** $6y + y + 8y$ **c** $m + 5m + 2m$
d $9p - 5p + 2p$ **e** $8u + 7u - 3u$ **f** $6k - k - 2k$

5 Simplify these expressions.

a $6d + 4d + 3$ **b** $7 + 3i + 2i$ **c** $10y - 2y + 9$
d $4p + 2p - 1$ **e** $7 + 7d - 2d$ **f** $6t - 2t + 5u$
g $9w - 3w + x$ **h** $c + 2c - d$ **i** $5e - e - 4f$

6 Simplify these expressions.

a $4q + 3q + 6i + i$ **b** $8z + 3z + 4b + 2b$
c $9u - 3u + 2v + 4v$ **d** $7j - 5j + 3k + 2k$
e $9m - 5m + 8n - 7n$ **f** $4d + 6d + 9 - 4$

1 i Write down the perimeter of each rectangle as simply as possible.
ii Write down the area of each rectangle as simply as possible.

a

3 cm

x cm

b
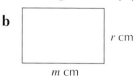

r cm

m cm

c
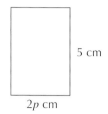

5 cm

2*p* cm

2 Write down the perimeter of each shape as simply as possible.

a
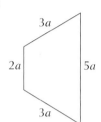

3*a*

2*a*   5*a*

3*a*

b
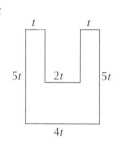

2*d*

7   5*d*

2*d*   5

3*d*

c

t   *t*

5*t*   2*t*   5*t*

4*t*

3 Write down the area of each shape as simply as possible.

a
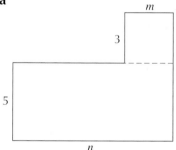

m

3

5

n

b
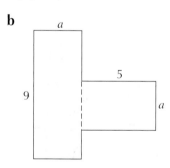

a

9   5

a

[**Hint:** Work out the area of each separate rectangle, then add them to get the total area.]

4 Choose one or more of the weights on the right that, together, will balance the weight on the left.

a
2*x* – 1
x + 2
x + 4
2*x* + 3

3*x* + 5

b
2*x* + 5
2*x* + 4
x + 2
3*x* – 2

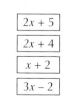
5*x* + 2

5E Expanding brackets

1 Expand these brackets.

a	$2(4 + 7)$	**b**	$5(9 - 4)$	**c**	$4(a + 3)$
d	$3(d + r)$	**e**	$2(3 - s)$	**f**	$4(b - 3)$
g	$5(2s + 3)$	**h**	$6(4 + 3i)$	**i**	$3(3u - 1)$
j	$6(4 - 5n)$				

2 Expand and simplify these expressions.

a	$6f + 4(f + 2)$	**b**	$2k + 3(k + 2)$	**c**	$4x + 2(2 + x)$
d	$3(m + 5) + 4m$	**e**	$5b + 2(3b + 1)$	**f**	$4(2g + 3) + g$

3 Expand and simplify these expressions.

a	$3(b + 2) - 4$	**b**	$3s + 4(s - 4)$	**c**	$5y + 2(3y - 1)$
d	$t + 2(t - u)$	**e**	$4n + 2(2n - m)$	**f**	$3(2r - 3n) + 2r$

CHAPTER 6
Geometry and Measures **2**

6A Perimeter and area of rectangles

1 **i** Calculate the perimeter of each rectangle.
   ii Calculate the area of each rectangle.

a

9 cm

7 cm

b

6 mm

12 mm

c

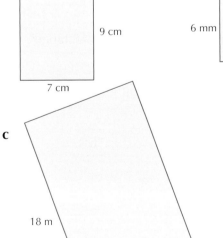

18 m

11 m

d

6 cm

1.6 cm

2 **i** Measure the sides of each rectangle to the nearest centimetre.
    ii Calculate the perimeter of each rectangle.
   iii Calculate the area of each rectangle.

a

b

c

3 This diagram shows the ground floor plan of a house.

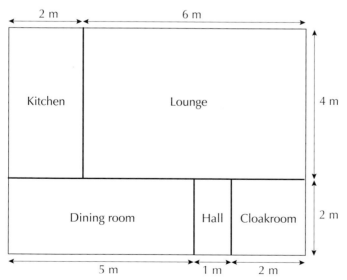

a Calculate the perimeter of each room, including the hall.
b Calculate the area of each room, including the hall.

4 On centimetre-squared paper, draw three different rectangles with an area of 24 cm².

1 Split each compound shape into rectangles as shown.
Find **i** the perimeter and **ii** the area of each shape.

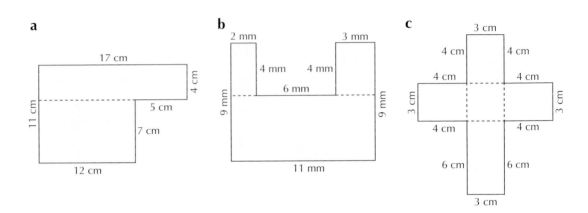

a   **b**   **c**

2 Copy each compound shape and find its missing sides.
Find the perimeter of each shape.

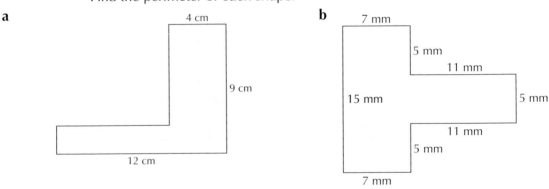

a   **b**

3 This diagram shows a piece of modern art.

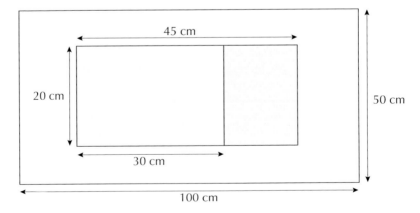

a Calculate the area that is yellow.
b Calculate the area that is green.
c Calculate the area that is white.
[**Hint:** Subtract the yellow and green areas from the area of the picture.]

6C Reading scales

1 **i** Calculate the size of each division on these number lines.

 ii Write down the number to which each arrow is pointing.

a

b
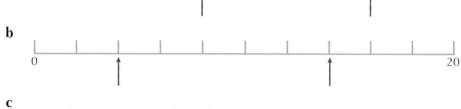

c

2 Measure the length of each object **i** in millimetres and **ii** in centimetres.

a

b

c
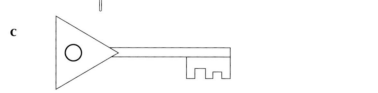

3 Write down the weight shown on each spring balance.

a
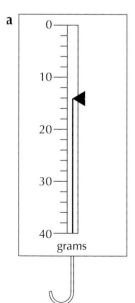

b
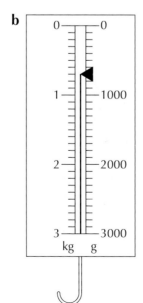

c
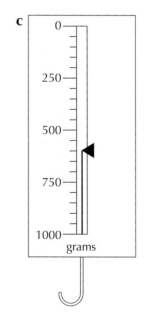

4 The scale shows the heights of different towns above sea level.
A negative height means the town is below sea level.

a Make a table to show the heights of the towns.

b Which town is 60 m lower than 220 m?

c Which town is 40 m lower than −20 m?

d Which town is 100 m higher than −280 m?

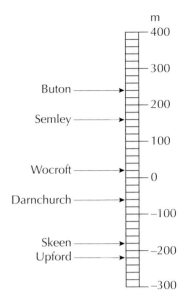

Practice

6D Surface area of cubes and cuboids

1 Find the surface area of cubes with these edge lengths.

   a 3 cm   **b** 6 cm   **c** 12 cm

2 Find the surface area of each cuboid.

a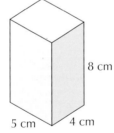

b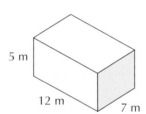

c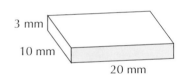

3 Calculate the total surface area of the inside and outside of this box, including the door. (Ignore the thickness of wood.)

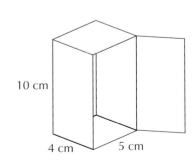

6E Converting one metric unit to another

1 Change each of these lengths to millimetres.

    a 8 cm   **b** 2.4 cm   **c** 0.7 cm   **d** 11.3 cm

2 Change each of these lengths to centimetres.

    a 40 mm   **b** 25 mm   **c** 72 mm
    d 160 mm   **e** 243 mm   **f** 6 mm

3 Change each of these lengths to centimetres.

    a 4 m   **b** 1.5 m   **c** 7.3 m
    d 0.6 m   **e** 0.14 m   **f** 0.03 m

4 Change each of these lengths to metres.

    a 800 cm   **b** 450 cm   **c** 223 cm
    d 76 cm   **e** 6 cm

5 Change each of these lengths to metres.

    a 9 km   **b** 6.4 km   **c** 0.8 km
    d 2.156 km   **e** 0.06 km

6 Change each of these lengths to kilometres.

    a 7000 m   **b** 9500 m   **c** 2300 m
    d 300 m   **e** 70 m

7 Change each of these capacities **i** to centilitres and **ii** to millilitres.

    a 3 l   **b** 5.5 l   **c** 0.8 l   **d** 9.3 l

8 Change each of these capacities to litres.

    a 6000 ml   **b** 200 cl   **c** 90 cl
    d 4500 ml   **e** 6 cl

CHAPTER 7 Algebra 3

7A Linear functions

1 **a** Copy this mapping diagram.

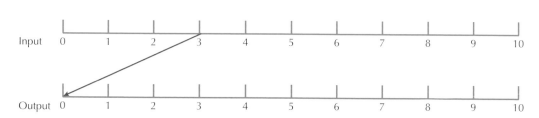

Input   0   1   2   3   4   5   6   7   8   9   10

Output   0   1   2   3   4   5   6   7   8   9   10

b Map the integer values from 3 to 10 for the function → subtract 3 →

c On your diagram, map these input values.

    i 5.5   **ii** 8.5   **iii** 4.5   **iv** 3.5

(2) a For each of these functions, use two number lines from 0 to 15 to draw a mapping diagram.

    i → multiply by 2 →   **ii** → add 4 →   **iii** → divide by 2 →

b On diagrams **i** and **ii**, map the values 3.5, 0.5 and 7.5.

(3) a Use two number lines from 0 to 10 to draw a mapping diagram for each of these functions.

    i → add 1 →

    ii → subtract 1 →

    iii → multiply by 3 →

b On diagrams **i** and **ii**, map the values 3.5, 1.5 and 4.5.

Practice

7B Finding a function from its inputs and outputs

(1) Find the function that maps these inputs to their respective outputs.

Each function is either → add → or → subtract →

a {1, 2, 3, 4} → {7, 8, 9, 10}

b {3, 4, 5, 6} → {1, 2, 3, 4}

c {0, 2, 4, 6} → {5, 7, 9, 11}

d {10, 15, 20, 25} → {0, 5, 10, 15}

(2) Find the function that maps these inputs to their respective outputs.

Each function is either → multiply → or → divide →

a {1, 2, 3, 4} → {5, 10, 15, 20}

b {4, 8, 12, 16} → {2, 4, 6, 8}

c {0, 10, 20, 30} → {0, 1, 2, 3}

d {0, 3, 5, 7} → {0, 9, 15, 21}

(3) Find the function that maps these inputs to their respective outputs.

a {1, 2, 3, 4} → {0, 1, 2, 3}

b {5, 6, 7, 8} → {15, 18, 21, 24}

c {6, 8, 10, 12} → {2, 4, 6, 8}

d {6, 9, 12, 15} → {2, 3, 4, 5}

e {3, 8} → {8, 13}

f {4, 7} → {24, 42}

(4) Write down two different functions that map the input 2 to the output 10.

7C Graphs from functions

1 Write these functions starting $y =$

Example   → | add 3 | →

Answer $y = x + 3$

a → | subtract 2 | →   **b** → | multiply by 4 | →

c → | add 7 | →   **d** → | multiply by 3 | →

e → | subtract 10 | →   **f** → | divide by 2 | →

2 a Copy and complete this table for the function $y = x + 5$.

x	0	1	2	3	4	5
$y = x + 5$						

b Draw a grid with its x-axis from 0 to 5 and y-axis from 0 to 10.
c Draw the graph of the function $y = x + 5$.

3 a Copy and complete this table for the function $y = x - 3$.

x	0	1	2	3	4	5	6
$y = x - 3$							

b Draw a grid with its x-axis from 0 to 6 and y-axis from −5 to 5.
c Draw the graph of the function $y = x - 3$.

4 a Copy and complete this table for each of the functions.

x	0	1	2	3	4	5
$y = x$						
$y = 2x$						
$y = 3x$						
$y = 4x$						

b Draw a grid with its x-axis from 0 to 5 and y-axis from 0 to 20.
c Draw the graph of each function in the table using the same grid.
d What is different about the lines?
e Use a dotted line to sketch the graph of $y = 2.5x$.

7D Rules with coordinates

Mario has lots of one centimetre square tiles, with a diamond in the top
right corner. He places the tiles in a row on a coordinate grid.

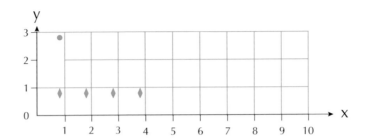

He writes down the coordinates of the corners with a ◆.
The corner of the first tile with a ◆ is (1, 1).

1 What are the coordinates of the corner with a ◆ on the 8th tile?

2 What are the coordinates of the corner with a ◆ on the *n*th tile?

3 Mario has lots of tiles like the one on the right.
These are placed in a row on top of the 1cm tiles.

a What are the coordinates of the corner with a • on the 5th tile?
b What are the coordinates of the corner with a • on the *n*th tile?

Practice

7E Distance–time graphs

1 Mrs Jay had to travel to a job interview at Penford 120 miles away.
She caught the 0900 train from Shobton and travelled to Deely, 30 miles away. This train journey took one hour.
There she had to wait 30 minutes for a connecting train to Penford. This train took $1\frac{1}{2}$ hours.
Her job interview at Penford lasted 2 hours.
Her return journey to Shobton lasted $1\frac{1}{2}$ hours.

a Copy this grid, using 2 cm to 1 hour and 1 cm to 10 miles.

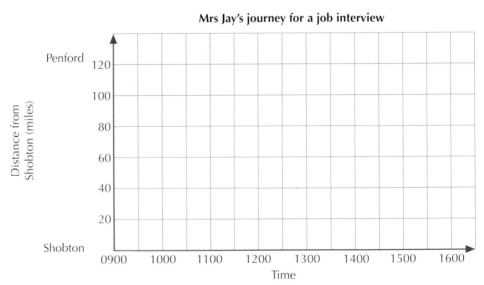

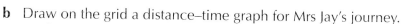

b Draw on the grid a distance–time graph for Mrs Jay's journey.
c Mark Deely on the vertical axis.
d How far was Mrs Jay from Shobton at 1130?
e At which times was Mrs Jay 60 miles from Shobton?

2 A petrol tanker made this journey along a motorway.

- Filled up at petrol depot.
- Drove 10 miles in 30 minutes to Dibley Sevices.
  Spent 30 minutes filling the pumps.
- Drove a further 20 miles in 1 hour to Penton Sevices.
  Spent 30 minutes filling the pumps and 30 minutes for a tea break.
- Drove a further 30 miles in 1 hour to Hillview Sevices.
  Spent 30 minutes filling the pumps.
- Returned to the depot in 90 minutes.

a Draw a grid with the following scales:
Horizontal axis (time), from 0 to 6 hours, 1 cm to 30 minutes
Vertical axis (distance), from 0 to 60 miles, 1 cm to 5 miles
b Draw on the grid a distance–time graph for the journey.
Mark the places of delivery on the vertical axis.
c How far was the tanker from the depot after:
i 90 minutes   **ii** 3.5 hours   **iii** 5 hours?

CHAPTER 8 Number 3

8A Powers of 10

Do not use your calculator.

1 Multiply each of these numbers **i** by 10 **ii** by 1000 and **iii** by 100.

a 2.7   **b** 0.05   **c** 38   **d** 0.008

2 Divide each of these numbers **i** by 10 **ii** by 1000 and **iii** by 100.

a 730   **b** 4   **c** 2.8   **d** 35 842

3 Calculate each of these.

a 7.4×1000 **b** $13 \times 100\,000$
c $0.87 \div 1000$ **d** $17.4 \div 100$
e 0.0065×1000 **f** $19.4 \div 10\,000$

④ Work your way along this chain of calculations for each of these starting numbers.

a 2000   **b** 7   **c** 0.06

i

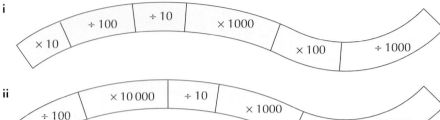

× 10 | ÷ 100 | ÷ 10 | × 1000 | × 100 | ÷ 1000

ii

÷ 100 | × 10 000 | ÷ 10 | × 1000 | ÷ 10 | ÷ 10 000

⑤ Round these numbers to 1 decimal place.

a 8.265   **b** 6.849   **c** 3.965
d 0.095   **e** 4.994   **f** 0.047

⑥ Round these numbers **i** to the nearest whole number and **ii** to 1 decimal place.

a 7.32   **b** 8.75   **c** 3.04
d 19.58   **e** 0.749   **f** 9.955

Practice

8B Large numbers

① Write these numbers in words.

a 956 348   **b** 15 230 421   **c** 8 002 040   **d** 604 500 002

② Write these numbers using figures.

a Ninety-two thousand and fifty-six
b Two hundred and six thousand, one hundred and seven
c Five million, thirty-two thousand and eight

③ This graph shows the numbers of oil shares sold every hour during a trading day.

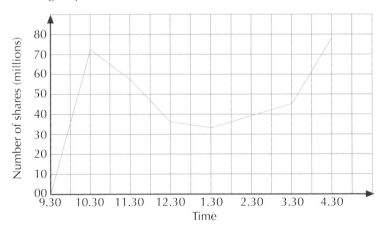

Estimate the number sold each hour. Make a table for your answers.

4 Round these numbers to the nearest **i** thousand **ii** ten thousand **iii** million.

a 7247 964   b 1952 599   c 645 491   d 9595 902

 5 The top six UK airports, in 2006, measured by number of passengers are shown in the table below.

1	Heathrow	67 339 000
2	Gatwick	34 080 000
3	Stansted	23 680 000
4	Manchester	22 124 000
5	Luton	9 415 000
6	Birmingham	9 056 000

a Which two of these airports had the same number of passengers to the nearest million?

b How many passengers used Heathrow, Gatwick or Stansted in 2006? Give your answer to the nearest ten million passengers.

Practice

8C Estimations

1 Explain why these calculations must be wrong.

a $53 \times 21 = 1111$ b $58 \times 34 = 2972$ c $904 \div 14 = 36$

2 Estimate answers to each of these calculations.

a $6832 - 496$ b 28×123 c $521 \div 18$

d 770×770 e $\dfrac{58.9 + 36.4}{22.5}$

3 Which is the best estimate for 15.4×21.6?

a 16×22 b 15×21 c 15×22 d 16×21

 4 a Football socks cost £3.71 a pair.
Without working out the correct answer, could Ian buy 5 pairs using a £20 note? Explain your answer.

b Shoelaces cost 68p a pair. The shopkeeper charged Ian £3.25 for 5 pairs. Without working out the correct answer, explain why is this incorrect.

5 Estimate the number to which each arrow is pointing.

a
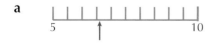

b

c

Do not use a calculator. Show your working.

1 Calculate each of these.

a   5.7 + 2.1
c   5.6 + 9.1 – 2.3
e   2 m + 4.6 m – 3.5 m

b   8.3 – 4.5
d   4.8 + 7.1 – 5.4
f   3.9 cm + 5.6 cm – 6.4 cm

2 Calculate each of these.

a   4.76 + 8.39
c   5.28 – 3.75
e   78.02 – 23.7 – 19.08
g   13 + 91.03 – 2.37

b   2.06 + 9.77 + 12.3
d   0.87 + 1.79 – 0.94
f   9.23 – 2.07 – 1.8

3 Calculate these. Work in metres.

a   5 m – 2.56 m + 108 cm
c   6 cm + 0.67 m – 0.09 m

b   0.95 m + 239 cm – 1.86 m
d   23 cm + 0.08 m – 7 cm

4 **a** Calculate the total volume of juice in these full bottles. Work in litres.
(**Remember:** 1 litre = 100 cl = 1000 ml.)

b All the juice is made into a fruit cocktail. Three cups are drunk. If a cup holds 15 cl, how much fruit cocktail is left? Work in litres.

5 The skin is the largest organ in the body and weighs 10.88 kg, on average. The four next largest organs are the liver (1.56 kg), brain (1.41kg), lungs (1.09 kg) and the heart (0.32 kg).

a Calculate the total weight of these four organs.
b How much more does the skin weigh than the total weight of the liver, brain, lungs and heart?

8E Efficient calculations

1 Without using a calculator, work out the value of these.

a $\dfrac{20 - 6}{2 + 5}$　　　　　　　　**b** $\dfrac{7 + 9}{0.9 - 0.4}$

2 Use a calculator to do the calculations in Question 1.
Are your answers the same as before?

3 For each part of Question 2, write down the sequence of keys that you pressed.

4 Work out the value of these. Round your answers to 1 decimal place, if necessary.

a $\dfrac{689 + 655}{100 - 58}$　　　　　　　　**b** $\dfrac{420 - 78}{54 \div 3}$

c $\dfrac{36 \times 84}{29 + 17}$　　　　　　　　**d** $\dfrac{296 + 112}{183 - 159}$

5 **a** Estimate the answer to: $\dfrac{443 - 178}{53 - 27}$

　　b Now use a calculator to work out the answer correct to 1 decimal place. Is your answer about the same?

6 Calculate these.

a $\sqrt{344\,569}$　　　　**b** 5.4^2
c $\sqrt{50.6 + 39.65}$　　**d** $(12.3 - 2.6)^2$

8F Long multiplication and long division

1 Work out each of the following multiplication and division problems. Use any method you are happy with.

　　a 17×4　　　**b** 46×6　　　**c** $76 \div 4$　　　**d** $95 \div 5$

2 Work out these long multiplication problems. Use any method you are happy with.

　　a 13×32　　　**b** 54×27　　　**c** 19×275　　　**d** 148×38

3 Work out these long division problems. Use any method you are happy with. Some of the problems will have a remainder.

　　a $420 \div 12$　　　**b** $600 \div 22$　　　**c** $738 \div 38$　　　**d** $884 \div 26$

For Questions 3–6, decide whether these problems are long multiplication or long division. Then do the appropriate calculation, showing your method clearly.

4 A sports stadium has 23 rows of seats. Each row has 84 seats. How many people can be seated in the stadium?

 5 A bag contains 448 g of flour. The flour is used to make cakes. Each cake contains 14 g of flour.

    a How many cakes were made?

    b How much flour is needed to make 234 cakes?

 6 An oven can bake 24 pizzas at a time. Each batch takes 11 minutes to cook.

    a How many pizzas could be baked in 3 hours?

    b How long would it take to bake 540 pizzas, in minutes?

    c Convert your answer to part **b** to hours and minutes.

 7 Floor tiles measure 35 cm by 26 cm. They cover a floor measuring 945 cm by 660 cm.

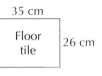

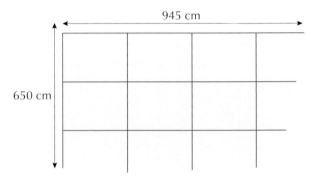

    a How many tiles are next to the long edge of the floor?

    b How many tiles are next to the short edge of the floor?

    c How many tiles were used to cover the floor?

CHAPTER 9 Geometry and Measures **3**

1 Use your ruler to check which of these triangles are congruent. Write your answer like this, e.g. A = D.

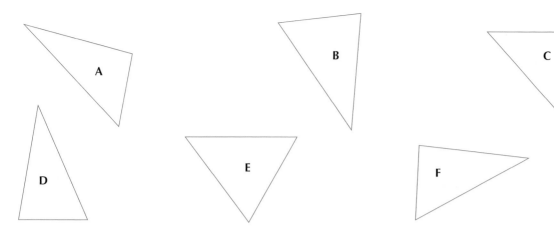

2 Which of these shapes are congruent?
Write your answer like this, e.g. A = D = F.

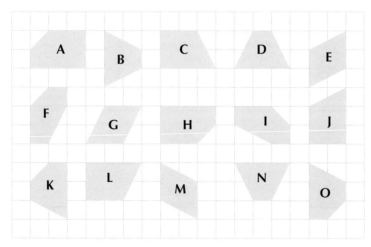

3 **a** Draw 15 shapes by joining some of the dots shown in the diagram.
Label your shapes from A to N. Two examples are shown.

b Write down the shapes that are congruent.

1 **a** Describe the single transformation that maps:

    i A on to F
    ii D on to A
    iii C on to A
    iv E on to F
    v D on to B

  b Describe a combination of two transformations that maps:

    i A on to D
    ii B on to C
    iii E on to G

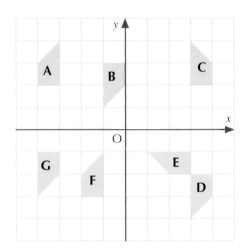

2 **a** Copy this diagram onto squared paper.
  b Reflect shape A in the dotted line. Label the image B.
  c Reflect shape B in the x-axis. Label the image C.
  d What single transformation maps shape A on to shape C?

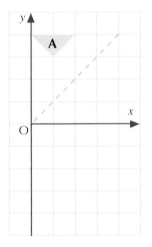

3 **a** Copy this diagram onto squared paper.
  b Reflect shape A in the y-axis. Label the image B.
  c Reflect shape B in the x-axis. Label the image C.

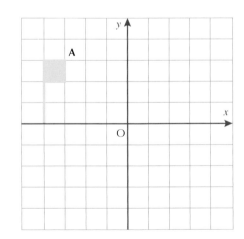

Practice

9C Reflections in two mirror lines

1. Copy each of the following shapes onto squared paper and reflect it in both mirror lines shown.

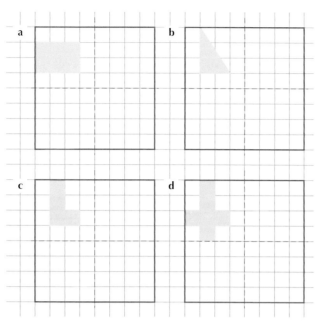

Practice

9D Shape and ratio

Express all ratio answers in their simplest form.

1. Express each of these ratios in its simplest form.

   a 90 cm : 20 cm   **b** 24 mm : 32 mm   **c** 150 cm : 2 m
   d 3 cm : 40 mm   **e** 0.5 km : 800 m

2.

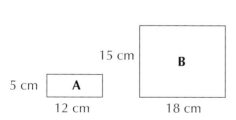

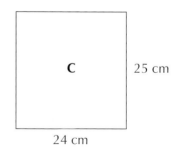

   a Find the ratio of the base of rectangle A to rectangle B.
   b **i** Calculate the areas of rectangles A and B.
      ii Find the ratio of the area of rectangle A to rectangle B.
   c **i** Calculate the area of rectangle C.
      ii Find the ratio of the area of rectangle B to rectangle C.

3 This diagram shows the design of a new flag.

    a Calculate the areas of green and white material.

    b Calculate the ratio of the green area to the white area.

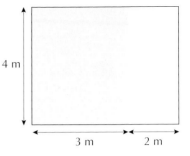

4 This diagram shows the plan of a garden.

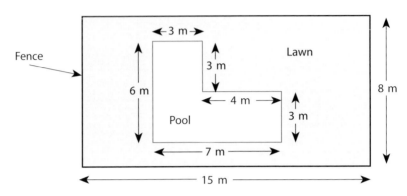

a Calculate the perimeter of the fence.

b Calculate the perimeter of the pool.

c Find the ratio of the perimeter of the fence to the perimeter of the pool.

CHAPTER 10 Algebra **4**

Practice

10A Solving equations and mapping

1 Solve these mappings.

  a $x \to \boxed{+4} \to 9$ **b** $a \to \boxed{\times 3} \to 21$ **c** $m \to \boxed{-6} \to 11$

  d $p \to \boxed{\div 3} \to 9$ **e** $n \to \boxed{-2} \to 25$ **f** $r \to \boxed{+8} \to 40$

2 Copy and complete these solutions to mappings.

  a $x \to \boxed{} \to 9$
          b $d \to \boxed{} \to 28$

    $? \leftarrow \boxed{+5} \leftarrow ?$
          $? \leftarrow \boxed{\div 4} \leftarrow ?$

    $x =$
              $d =$

  c $n \to \boxed{} \to 6$
          d $p \to \boxed{} \to 27$

    $? \leftarrow \boxed{\times 3} \leftarrow ?$
         $19 \leftarrow \boxed{} \leftarrow ?$

    $n =$
             $p =$

3 Solve these equations.
Write each equation as a mapping. Then solve the mapping.

  a $c - 2 = 7$ **b** $4w = 36$ **c** $q + 13 = 18$

  d $6d = 48$ **e** $\frac{u}{2} = 7$ **f** $V - 11 = 17$

Practice

10B Equations and mappings involving two operations

1 Solve these mappings.

  a $m \to \boxed{\times 2} \to \boxed{+ 4} \to 10$ **b** $d \to \boxed{\times 4} \to \boxed{- 7} \to 13$

  c $k \to \boxed{\times 9} \to \boxed{+ 7} \to 25$ **d** $t \to \boxed{\times 4} \to \boxed{- 16} \to 20$

  e $e \to \boxed{\times 3} \to \boxed{- 11} \to 1$ **f** $r \to \boxed{\times 5} \to \boxed{- 32} \to 23$

2 Copy and complete these mappings.

  a $b \to \boxed{} \to \boxed{- 4} \to 11$

     $? \leftarrow \boxed{+ 5} \leftarrow \boxed{} \leftarrow ?$

     $b =$

  b $s \to \boxed{\times 4} \to \boxed{} \to 18$

     $? \leftarrow \boxed{} \leftarrow \boxed{- 6} \leftarrow ?$

     $s =$

  c $f \to \boxed{} \to \boxed{- 4} \to 6$

     $5 \leftarrow \boxed{} \leftarrow \boxed{} \leftarrow ?$

     $f =$

3 Write a mapping for each problem. Then solve the mapping.

a If I multiply my number by n by 6 then subtract 5, the answer is 19. What is n?

b If I multiply my number by n by 4 then subtract y, the answer is 3. What is n?

c If I multiply my number by n by 5 then add 13, the answer is 48. What is n?

d If I multiply my number by n by 12 then add 9, the answer is 45. What is n?

Practice

10C Solving equations

1 **i** Write the equation that is given by each of the following mappings.
  ii Use inverse mapping to solve each equation.

  a $x \to \boxed{\times 3} \to \boxed{- 2} \to 13$

  b $x \to \boxed{\div 2} \to \boxed{+ 3} \to 8$

  c $x \to \boxed{\times 4} \to \boxed{+ 6} \to 16$

2 **i** Draw the mapping diagram for each of the following equations.
   ii Use inverse mapping to solve each equation.

   a $2x - 5 = 9$ **b** $4x - 1 = 15$ **c** $3x + 2 = 11$

3 To solve these equations, write each equation as a mapping.
   Then solve the mapping.

   a $4x + 3 = 15$ **b** $5y - 4 = 6$ **c** $2t - 13 = 5$
   d $6p + 7 = 31$ **e** $9k + 3 = 21$ **f** $10r - 16 = 24$

Practice

10D Substituting into expressions

1 Write down the value of each expression for each value of x.

		i	**ii**	**iii**
a	$4x$ when	$x = 2$	$x = 7$	$x = -3$
b	$p + 2$ when	$p = 4$	$p = 0$	$p = -10$
c	$4d + 3$ when	$d = 2$	$d = 6$	$d = 20$
d	$2s - 3$ when	$s = 3$	$s = 10$	$s = 50$
e	$\frac{m}{3}$ when	$m = 6$	$m = 30$	$m = -24$
f	$3n - 2$ when	$n = 2$	$n = 0$	$n = 100$

2 If $p = 3$ and $q = 5$, find the value of each of these.

   a $2q - p$ **b** $q + 3p$ **c** $3p - q$

3 If $r = 2$ and $s = 3$, find the value of each of these.

   a $r - s$ **b** $r - 2s$ **c** $2r + 3s$

4 If $x = 3$, $y = 5$ and $z = 2$ find the value of each of these.

   a xyz **b** $y + z - x$ **c** $xz + y$ **d** $2x + 3y + 4z$

Practice

10E Substituting into formulae

1 The cost of a sheet of glass is given by the formula $C = 3bh$ where C is the cost (£), b the breadth and h the height in metres.
Calculate the cost of sheets of glass with these dimensions.

   a breadth 2 m, height 4 m   **b** breadth 5 m, height 1 m
   c breadth 4 m, height 2.5 m

2 Given that $C = F + 4d$, find the value of C when:

    a $F = 12, d = 6$ **b** $F = 20, d = 15$ **c** $F = 100, d = 200$

3 **a** The weight, W g of a pack of sausages is given by the formula $W = 50n$, where n is the number of sausages in the pack.
Calculate the weight of a pack containing:

    i   6 sausages   **ii**   10 sausages   **iii**   18 sausages

    b The weight, W g of a barbecue pack of sausages and burgers is given by the formula $W = 50n + 100m$, where n is the number of sausages and m is the number of burgers in the pack.
Calculate the weight of a pack when:

    i $n = 6, m = 4$ **ii** $n = 8, m = 8$ **iii** $n = 14, m = 15$

4 The average, A, of three numbers m, n and p is given by the formula

$$A = \frac{m + n + p}{3}$$

Calculate the value of W when:

    a $m = 4, n = 2, p = 6$ **b** $m = 5, n = 11, p = 11$
    c $m = 15, n = 15, p = 45$

5 The approximate area of a circle of radius r is given by the formula $A = 3 \times r \times r$, where A is the area and r is the radius.

Find the area of a circle of radius:

    a   5 cm   **b**   9 cm   **c**   20 cm

Practice

10F Creating your own expressions

1 Write an expression for each of these using the letters suggested.

    a The sum of the numbers d and 3.
    b The number u reduced by 5.
    c The product of the numbers w, 7 and s.
    d One third of the number m.
    e The number of toes on f feet.

2 **a** How many months are there in Y years?
    b How many metres are there in x centimetres?

3 Michael is H cm tall now.

    a He was 5 cm shorter a year ago. How tall was he then?
    b In 3 years time, he will be x cm taller. How tall will he be then?

Michael's taller sister Briony is S cm tall.

c How much taller is Briony than Michael?

d What is the average height of Michael and Briony?

4 a A Chocolate Wheel costs c pence and a Frother costs f pence.
What is the total cost of:
  i a Chocolate Wheel and a Frother
  ii 5 Frothers
  iii 3 Chocolate Wheels and 2 Frothers?
b How much change from a £2 coin would you receive for each of the purchases in part **a**?

CHAPTER **11** Statistics **2**

1 The table below shows the distances, in miles, between service stations on the motorways:

Bramich				
58	Exline			
114	64	Hopewell		
87	65	53	Newbridge	
140	122	83	59	Sheepster

a How far apart are Exline and Newbridge?

b How far apart are Bramich and Hopewell?

c Which service station is 122 miles from Exline?

d Which two service stations are furthest from each other?

e How much further away from Bramich is Sheepster than Hopewell?

2 Five friends try to organise an evening when they can all play a new computer game together. The table shows who is able to play on which nights:

	Mon	Tue	Wed	Thur	Fri	Sat	Sun
Andy	√	√		√			√
Dave		√	√	√	√	√	
Kev	√			√		√	√
Siad				√	√		√
Terry	√	√	√	√		√	

a   On which days can Andy play?
b   Who is available to play on Friday?
c   Which is the night they can all play?
d   Three of the friends got together on Tuesday night and one of them damaged the computer game. What is the probability that the person damaging the computer game was:
   i   Dave
   ii   Siad?

3   This table shows some information about pupils starting and leaving a school from 2004 to 2007:

	Number starting the school		Number leaving the school	
	Boys	**Girls**	**Boys**	**Girls**
2004	130	145	85	75
2005	138	142	99	65
2006	137	145	120	110
2007	150	135	125	85

a   How many started the school in 2006?
b   How many more started the school in 2004 than left it?
c   Which year had the biggest difference in numbers starting and leaving?
d   Did the number of pupils leaving the school increase each year? Explain your answer

4   The following table shows some information about pupils in a Year 8 class:

Hair colour	Number of boys	Number of girls
Black	8	3
Brown	7	2
Light	2	8

a   How many pupils are in the class?
b   How many of the pupils have black hair?
c   One pupil in the class is chosen at random. What is the probability that this pupil:
   i   has light hair
   ii   is a girl with black hair
   iii   is a girl?

4

1 The diagram shows the hours spent on a day's shifts at a hospital for a team of radiographers:

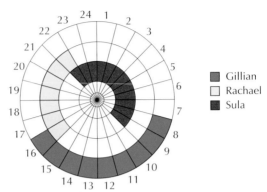

■ Gillian
□ Rachael
■ Sula

a Who works the most hours?
b Who works the least hours?
c Sula says, 'I work for half the day here.'
Is Sula correct? Explain your answer.

2 The diagram shows the time that Mia spent one day on certain activities:

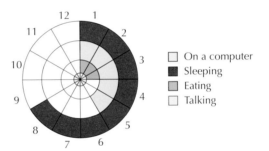

□ On a computer
■ Sleeping
■ Eating
□ Talking

a How many hours does Mia spend:
i on a computer ii talking iii sleeping iv eating?
b What suggests that Mia talks while doing other things?

3 The diagram shows the months that various plants are in bloom:

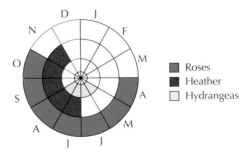

■ Roses
■ Heather
□ Hydrangeas

a For how many months in the year:
   i do roses bloom? ii does heather bloom?
b Max says, 'Hydrangeas bloom for a third of a year.'
Is he right? Explain your answer.

1 1200 pupils in a school were asked to vote for their favourite teacher.
The pie chart illustrates their responses:

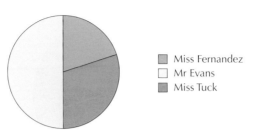

Miss Fernandez
Mr Evans
Miss Tuck

How many voted for:
a Miss Fernandez   **b** Mr Evans   **c** Miss Tuck?

2 One day at a park cafe, they sold 600 sandwiches.
The pie chart illustrates the different type that were sold:

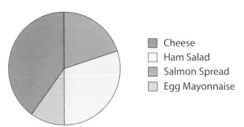

Cheese
Ham Salad
Salmon Spread
Egg Mayonnaise

How many of the following sandwiches were sold that weekend:
a cheese   **b** ham salad   **c** salmon spread
d egg mayonnaise?

3 The pie chart illustrates how many of the 24 absences a class had one week
were distributed on the different days of the week:

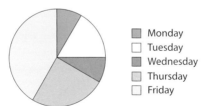

Monday
Tuesday
Wednesday
Thursday
Friday

How many pupils were absent on:
a Monday   **b** Tuesday   **c** Wednesday
d Thursday   **e** Friday?

4 Mona carried out a survey on how often people in her school ate
chocolate. She asked 80 people.
The pie chart illustrates her results:
How many of these people:
a never ate chocolate?
b ate chocolate once a week?
c ate chocolate occasionally?
d ate chocolate every day?

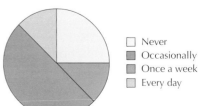

Never
Occasionally
Once a week
Every day

5

1 The pie chart shows the percentage of people of different ages at a cricket match:

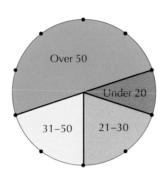

What percentage of people at the cricket match were aged:
a under 20   **b** 21 to 30   **c** 31 to 50   **e** over 50?

2 The pie chart shows the percentage of birds seen in a London garden one weekend:

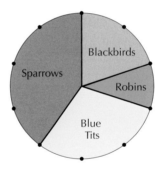

What percentage of birds were:
a sparrows   **b** blackbirds   **c** blue tits   **e** robins?

3 The pie chart shows the percentage of various school outings that pupils chose as their favourite:

What percentage of the students said their favourite outing was:
a a theme park   **b** the seaside   **c** a museum   **d** a historical site?

4 The pie chart shows the percentage of various detectives shows on TV that pupils' parents chose as their favourite:

What percentage of the students said their parent's favourite detective was:
a Inspector Morse **b** A Touch of Frost **c** Poirot
d Waking the Dead?

5 The pie chart shows the percentage of various age groups at a Bob Dylan concert:

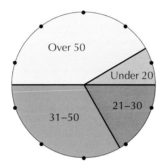

What percentage of the people at the concert were aged:
a under 20 **b** 21–30 **c** 31–50 **d** over 50?

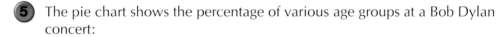

Practice

11E Information from other diagrams

1 A teacher created a diagram showing how two classes had performed in their Y8 Christmas assessment and their Y8 Easter assessment:

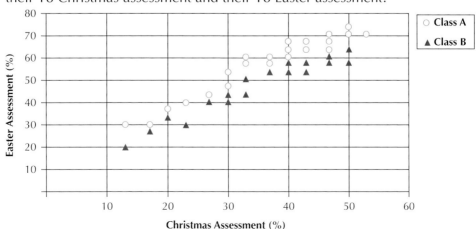

a How many pupils scored less than 40% at Christmas but higher than 50% at Easter?

b Which group showed most improvement?

c How many pupils in each group gained more than 60% at Easter?

2 A school made estimates of the numbers of pupils expected to get each Key Stage 3 level. The bar chart shows the estimated results and the actual results for the pupils:

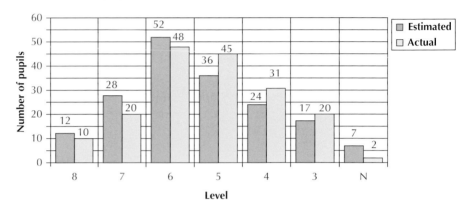

a For which grades did the pupils do better than the school estimated?

b How many pupils:
   i were expected to get a level 4 or 5
   ii actually got a level 4 or 5?

c What level showed the greatest difference between expected results and actual results?

3 The pie chart shows the number of pupils in a school choosing different activities during a sports day:

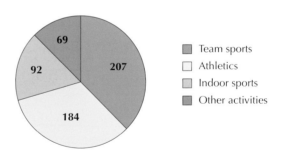

a How many pupils took part in the activities?

b Approximately, what fraction of pupils chose:
   i team sports   **ii** athletics   **iii** indoor sports?

CHAPTER 12 Number 4

Practice

12A Fractions

1 Copy and complete each of these.

a $\frac{9}{4} = \frac{\square}{12}$

b $\frac{20}{3} = \frac{180}{\square}$

c $\frac{11}{2} = \frac{99}{\square}$

d $\frac{32}{7} = \frac{\square}{35}$

e $\frac{100}{28} = \frac{\square}{7}$

f $\frac{144}{60} = \frac{12}{\square}$

2 **a** How many fifths are in 1?
   b How many fifths are in 3?

3 **a** How many fifths are in $3\frac{4}{5}$?

   b How many thirds are in $7\frac{1}{3}$?

   c How many twelfths are in $4\frac{7}{12}$?

   d How many sevenths are in 9?

4 Convert these mixed numbers to top-heavy fractions.

a $1\frac{2}{3}$

b $3\frac{1}{8}$

c $2\frac{5}{6}$

d $5\frac{1}{4}$

e $9\frac{1}{2}$

f $6\frac{3}{10}$

5 Convert these decimals to fractions.

a 0.7

b 0.6

c 0.45

d 0.16

e 0.08

f 0.33

6 Convert each of these top-heavy fractions to a mixed number in its simplest form.

a $\frac{13}{5}$

b $\frac{32}{3}$

c $\frac{28}{9}$

d $\frac{40}{6}$

e $\frac{60}{8}$

f $\frac{84}{18}$

g $\frac{133}{21}$

h thirteen-thirds

i eighteen-eighths

7 What fraction of a litre is:

a 80 cl

b 55 cl

c 240 cl

d 700 ml

e 245 ml

f 3350 ml?

(**Remember:** 1 litre = 100 cl and 1 litre = 1000 ml.)

12B Adding and subtracting fractions

5

1 Find the lowest common multiple of these pairs of numbers.

a 2, 5 **b** 6, 8 **c** 2, 6
d 10, 15 **e** 9, 12

For Questions 2–4, convert the fractions to equivalent fractions with a common denominator. Then work out the answers. Cancel your answers and write them as mixed numbers if necessary.

6

2 **a** $\frac{2}{5} + \frac{1}{2}$ **b** $\frac{5}{8} + \frac{1}{12}$ **c** $\frac{5}{6} + \frac{1}{3}$ **d** $\frac{4}{7} + \frac{3}{5}$

3 **a** $\frac{3}{5} - \frac{1}{2}$ **b** $\frac{5}{9} - \frac{1}{6}$ **c** $\frac{7}{8} - \frac{2}{3}$ **d** $\frac{7}{10} - \frac{1}{4}$

3 **a** $\frac{3}{7} + \frac{2}{3}$ **b** $\frac{5}{12} + \frac{1}{8}$ **c** $\frac{7}{9} + \frac{5}{6}$

d $\frac{3}{5} + \frac{1}{2} + \frac{7}{10}$ **e** $\frac{7}{9} - \frac{1}{2}$ **f** $\frac{11}{15} - \frac{2}{5}$

g $\frac{5}{6} - \frac{1}{10}$ **h** $\frac{2}{3} + \frac{5}{6} - \frac{5}{12}$

12C Order of operations

5

Do not use a calculator. Show all of your working.

1 Write down the operation that you would do first in each of these calculations. Then calculate the answer.

a $12 - 3 \times 2$ **b** $2 \times (9 - 5)$ **c** $10 \times 2 \div 5 + 3$
d $30 - 20 + 10$ **e** $12 + 8 - 3^2$ **f** $4 \times (2 + 5)^2$

2 Calculate each of these. Show each step of your calculation.

a $3^2 + 5 \times 2$ **b** $10 - (1 + 2)^2$ **c** $3 \times 12 \div 3^2$

d $32 \div (3^2 - 1)$ **e** $\dfrac{60 + 12}{2 \times 3}$ **f** $\dfrac{60}{(6 + 3^2)}$

g $1.5 + 3 \times (2.4 - 0.8) - 2.1$

3 Copy each calculation. Insert brackets to make the answer true.

a $11 - 7 - 1 + 4 = 1$ **b** $1 + 4 + 3^2 = 50$
c $24 \div 2 \times 3 = 4$ **d** $6 + 9 \div 12 \div 4 = 5$
e $12 - 3^2 - 7 \times 4 = 4$

12D Multiplying decimals

Do not use a calculator.

1 Calculate these.

   a 0.6×7 **b** 0.9×9 **c** 0.5×5 **d** 0.2×3
   e 0.4×4 **f** 0.4×8 **g** 0.3×6 **h** 0.8×1

2 Calculate these.

   a 0.6×0.7 **b** 0.9×0.9 **c** 0.5×0.7 **d** 0.2×0.3
   e 0.4^2 **f** 0.4×0.9 **g** 0.3×0.6 **h** 0.8×0.1

3 Calculate these.

   a 0.3×0.04 **b** 0.09×0.4 **c** 0.06×0.06 **d** 0.007×0.2
   e 0.08×0.03 **f** 0.4×0.08 **g** 0.003×0.2 **h** 0.9×0.002

4 Calculate these.

   a 40×0.7 **b** 0.4×60 **c** 20×0.2 **d** 0.9×90

5 Calculate these.

   a 200×0.9 **b** 0.8×400 **c** 500×0.09
   d 2000×0.7 **e** 0.08×300 **f** 9000×0.004
   g 70×0.04 **h** 300×0.002

6 A seed weighs 0.04 g. How much do 600 seeds weigh?

7 Sound travels about 0.3 km in 1 second. How far does sound travel in

   a 200 seconds   **b** 600 seconds   **c** 0.1 seconds? Work in kilometres.

12E Dividing decimals

Do not use a calculator.

1 Work out these.

   a $0.6 \div 3$ **b** $0.8 \div 2$ **c** $0.36 \div 2$ **d** $0.9 \div 3$
   e $0.4 \div 1$ **f** $0.15 \div 3$ **g** $0.35 \div 5$ **h** $0.08 \div 2$

2 Calculate these.

   a $0.6 \div 0.3$ **b** $0.8 \div 0.2$ **c** $0.36 \div 0.2$ **d** $0.9 \div 0.3$
   e $0.4 \div 0.1$ **f** $0.15 \div 0.3$ **g** $0.35 \div 0.5$ **h** $0.08 \div 0.2$

3 Calculate these.

   a $9 \div 0.3$ **b** $40 \div 0.8$ **c** $60 \div 0.3$ **d** $48 \div 0.6$
   e $500 \div 0.2$ **f** $900 \div 0.3$ **g** $5000 \div 0.5$ **h** $120 \div 0.6$

4 Calculate these.

    a $0.8 \div 0.04$ **b** $0.6 \div 0.02$ **c** $0.48 \div 0.06$ **d** $0.16 \div 0.04$

5 Calculate these.

    a $30 \div 0.6$ **b** $600 \div 0.3$ **c** $20 \div 0.05$
    d $3000 \div 0.1$ **e** $80 \div 0.02$

6 £1 buys 0.05 g of platinum. How much does 4 g of platinum cost?

CHAPTER 13 Algebra 5

Practice

13A Expansion of brackets

1 Copy and complete each of the following.

    a $3(4 + 3) = 3 \times 7 = \square$
       $3 \times 4 + 3 \times 3 = 12 + \square = \square$
       $3(4 + 3) = 3 \times 4 + 3 \times 3$
    b $6(5 - 3) = 6 \times \square = \square$
       $6 \times 5 - 6 \times 3 = 30 - \square = \square$
       $6(5 - 3) = \square \times \square - \square \times \square$
    c $3(m + 1) = 3 \times m + 3 \times 1 = \square + \square$
    d $4(n - 3) = 4 \times \square - 4 \times \square = \square - \square$
    e $6(m + n) = \square \times \square + \square \times \square = \square + \square$

2 Expand each of the following.

    a $3(2 + t)$ **b** $6(x - 2)$ **c** $5(x + y)$
    d $2(t + 5)$ **e** $4(m - 3)$

3 Copy and complete each of the following.

    a $4(3m + 2) = 4 \times 3m + 4 \times 2 = \square + \square$
    b $5(2n - 1) = 5 \times \square - 5 \times \square = \square - \square$
    c $2(5m + 3n) = \square \times \square + \square \times \square = \square + \square$

Practice

13B Solving equations

1 Solve these equations. Write a mapping for each equation. Then solve the mapping.

    a $3t = 18$ **b** $4u = 32$ **c** $9p = 27$ **d** $2h = 13$
    e $y + 4 = 16$ **f** $m - 6 = 11$ **g** $x + 12 = 30$ **h** $m - 13 = 28$

2 Solve these equations. Write a mapping for each equation. Then solve the mapping.

a $2x + 5 = 11$　　　b $4y - 1 = 7$　　　c $3i + 7 = 25$
d $5n - 25 = 30$　　e $9u + 3 = 30$　　f $7k - 4 = 31$

3 Mary made some mistakes in her homework. Explain the mistakes and correct them.

a $c + 5 = 12$
　　$c \rightarrow +5 \rightarrow 12$
　　$17 \leftarrow +5 \leftarrow 12$
　　$c = 17$

b $4b - 8 = 16$
　　$b \rightarrow -8 \rightarrow \times 4 \rightarrow 16$
　　$12 \leftarrow +8 \leftarrow \div 4 \leftarrow 16$
　　$b = 12$

4 Expand the brackets first. Then solve the equation.

a $4(d + 3) = 32$　　b $4(t - 2) = 12$　　c $5(2s + 1) = 35$
d $3(2g + 10) = 60$　e $3(2f - 1) = 9$　　f $3(4q + 5) = 51$

Practice

13C Constructing equations to solve problems

1 Write down an algebraic expression for each of the following.

a The number which is 4 less than y.
b The number which is 5 times as large as x.
c The sum of a and b.
d The number that is double z.
e The product of p and q.

2 a A book and writing pad cost £8 altogether. The book costs £x.
　　Write an expression for the cost of the writing pad.
b Maria is twice as old as Janine. Janine is j years old.
　　Write an expression for Maria's age.
c The difference between the heights of two trees is 4 m. The taller tree is T metres high. Write an expression for the height of the shorter tree.

3 Solve these problems by creating an equation for each one and then solving it.

a Tyres cost £x each. 4 tyres cost £112.
　　Find the cost of one tyre.
b Jamie is y years old and Paul is 9 years old. Their ages total 16 years.
　　How old is Jamie?
c The difference between two numbers is 5.
　　The larger number is n and the smaller number is 12.
　　What is the larger number?
d A plum weighs p grams. A lemon weighs 12 g more than the plum.
　　i How much does the lemon weigh?
　　ii Write an expression for the total weight of the lemon and plum.
　　iii If the total weight is 44 g, find the weight of the plum.

e A soap opera lasts 3 times as long as a cartoon.
The cartoon lasts *m* minutes.
   i How long does the soap opera last?
   ii Write an expression for the total length of the two programmes.
   iii The soap opera and the cartoon last 32 minutes altogether.
       How long does the cartoon last?

13D Lines and equations

1 Write down the coordinates of the points on each dotted line.
Then write down the equation of the dotted line.

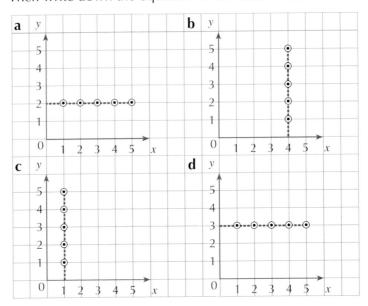

2 Use a grid to draw a graph for each of these equations.
Number the axes of your grids from 0 to 6.

   a $x = 4$ **b** $y = 6$ **c** $x = 2$ **d** $y = 1$

3

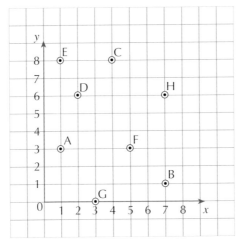

Write down the points that lie on each of these lines.
   a $y = 6$ **b** $x = 7$ **c** $y = 1$ **d** $x = 3$ **e** $y = 3$ **f** $x = 1$

4 **a** Draw a grid with each axis numbered from 0 to 6.
b **i** Mark four points on the *x*-axis and write down their coordinates.
ii Write down the equation of the *x*-axis.
c **i** Mark four points on the *y*-axis and write down their coordinates.
ii Write down the equation of the *y*-axis.

5 **i** Write down the coordinates of the marked points on each dotted line.

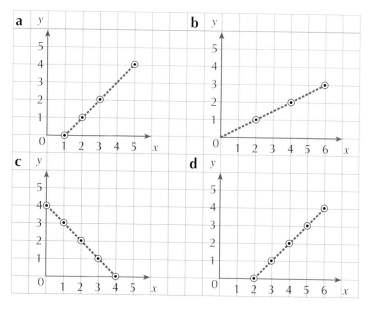

ii What is the rule connecting the *x*- and *y*-coordinates?
iii Use algebra to write your rule.

Practice

13E Real-life graphs

1 Match each of the three graphs shown to the situation that it illustrates.

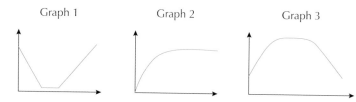

Graph 1   Graph 2   Graph 3

a The height of a person from birth to age 30 years
b The temperature in summer from midnight to midnight
c The height of water in a toilet cistern from before it is flushed to afterwards

2 This diagram shows the cost of car hire for two companies.

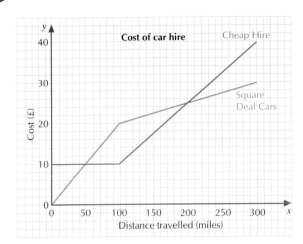

a Estimate the cost of hiring a car from each company and travelling
   i 60 miles
   ii 100 miles
   iii 240 miles
b When is Cheap Hire cheaper than Square Deal Cars?

3 Match each description to its graph.

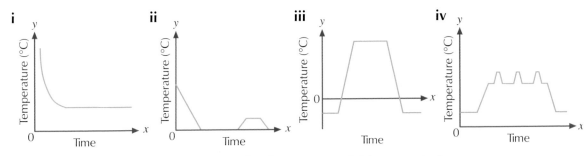

a The temperature of a desert over a 24-hour period
b The temperature of a kitchen over a 24-hour period
c The temperature of pond during a month of winter
d The temperature of a cup of tea as it cools down

4 George tried several diets to lose weight. This table shows his weight loss over a one-year period.

Diet	Weight loss/gain
Hay diet	Lost 10 kg in 2 months
Calorie counter	Stayed same weight for 3 months
Vegetarian	Gained 3 kg in 2 months
Usual diet	Gained 12 kg in 1 month
Atkins diet	Lost 28 kg in 4 months

George weighed 105 kg at the beginning of the year.

Draw a graph showing how George's weight changed over time.
Use the horizontal axis for time, with 1 cm to 1 month, from 0 to 12 months.
Use the vertical axis for weight, with 1 cm to 2 kg, from 80 kg to 112 kg.

CHAPTER 14 Solving Problems

Practice

14A Number and measures

1 Find two consecutive numbers that add up to 77.

2 Two consecutive numbers add up to 49. What are the numbers?

3 Two consecutive numbers add up to 57. What are the numbers?

4 Two consecutive numbers multiply together to give 42. What are the numbers?

5 Two consecutive numbers multiply together to give 110. What are the numbers?

6 Two consecutive numbers multiply together to give 72. What are the numbers?

Practice

14B Using algebra and diagrams to solve problems

1 I think of a number, treble it and then subtract 24. The answer is 27.

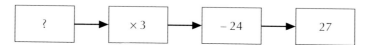

Work backwards to find the number I first thought of.

2 I think of a number, divide it by 2 and then add 8. The answer is 20.

a Copy and complete this flow diagram.

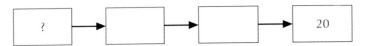

| ? | | | 20 |

b Work backwards to find the number I first thought of.

3 I think of a number, multiply by 3 and add 8. The answer is 20.

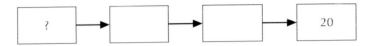

| ? | | | 20 |

Work backwards to find the number.

4 I think of a number, divide it by 2 and subtract 3. The answer is 3.

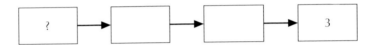

| ? | | | 3 |

Work backwards to find the number.

5 I am 18 years old.

a How old was I x years ago?
b Calculate my age 11 years ago.

6 There are about 30 grams in one ounce.

a Write a formula, in words, that changes a number of ounces into grams.
Number of grams =
b Copy and complete the formula to convert n ounces into G grams:
$G =$
c Use your formula to convert 14 ounces to grams.

Practice

14C Logic and proof

1 Copy and complete these number problems.

a
```
    2 □
+ □ 3
─────
  5 9
```

b
```
    7 □
+ 2 □ 5
───────
□ 9 9
```

c
```
  1 9 □
−  □ 2
───────
  1 3 2
```

d
```
    4 □
×  □ 9
───────
  3 8 7
```

2 Give some examples to show that the product of three odd numbers is odd.

(3) Give some examples to show that the product of two odd and two even numbers is even.

(4) **a** Write down the factors of 21.
   b Give another example to show that the factors of an odd number are odd.

(5) It takes 8 people 12 hours to dig a hole. How long would it take to dig the same hole if there were:

   a 4 people **b** 2 people **c** 16 people?

(6) Six glasses hold 120 cl altogether. Eight mugs hold 144 cl altogether. Which holds the most, a mug or a glass?

Practice

14D Proportion

(1) Two of the carriages on a train are first class. The other six carriages are standard class. A train franchise has 120 carriages altogether. How many are:

   a first class **b** standard class?

(2) A value pack contains 4 chocolate bars and 8 toffee bars. Nat buys some value packs and has 72 bars altogether. How many are:

   a chocolate bars **b** toffee bars?

(3) One out of every 10 people is left-handed.
In a group of 120 people, how many are likely to be left-handed?

(4) Air consists of 4 parts nitrogen to 1 part oxygen.
A cupboard contains 50 litres of air.

   a How much nitrogen does it contain?
   b How much oxygen does it contain?

(5) 9 light bulbs cost £18. How much does a box of 18 cost?

(6) 2 gallons is approximately 9 litres.

   a How many litres are equivalent to 10 gallons?
   b How many gallons are equivalent to 63 litres?

(7) 8 grams of silver are used to make 12 cm of chain.

   a How much silver does 36 cm of chain contain?
   b How long is a chain that contains 64 grams of silver?

Practice **14E Ratio**

5

1. Simplify these ratios.

   a 12 : 9 **b** 16 : 30 **c** 18 kg : 42 kg
   d £4 : 75p **e** 8 weeks : 12 days **f** 45 cm : 3 m
   g 5 kg : 1.75 kg

2. **a** Divide 40 cm in the ratio 7 : 1.
   b Divide 600 mm in the ratio 11 : 9.
   c Divide 5000 people in the ratio 3 : 5.
   d Divide £76 in the ratio 2 : 7 : 10.

3. Donna eats three times more hot meals than cold meals. She eats 96 meals in July. How many of them were hot?

4. The ratio of pupils in Year 8 who own a mobile phone to those that don't is 3 : 2. There are 210 pupils in Year 8.
   How many pupils do *not* own a mobile phone?

5. The land area to sea area of the surface of the Earth is in the ratio 3 : 7.
   The total surface area of the Earth is 500 000 000 km².
   What is the area of land?

CHAPTER **15** Geometry and Measures **4**

Practice **15A Plans and elevations**

5

1. For each of these 3-D shapes, draw on squared paper the:

   i plan **ii** front elevation **iii** side elevation

   a 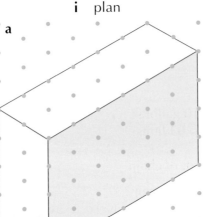 **b** 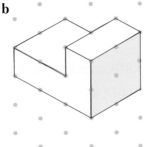 **c**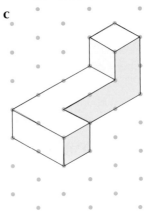

2 The plan, front and side elevations of a 3-D shape are shown below.
Draw the solid on an isometric grid.

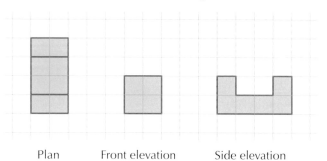

Plan   Front elevation   Side elevation

15B Scale drawings

1 These objects have been drawn using the scales shown.
Find the true lengths of the objects.

a

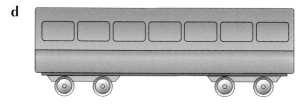

Scale

1 cm to 10 cm

b

2 cm to 1 m

c

1 cm to 0.7 m

d

2 cm to 3 m

FM **2** This diagram shows a scale drawing of an aircraft hangar.

Scale: 1 cm to 120 m

a) Calculate the real length of the hangar.
b) Calculate the real width of the hangar.
c) Calculate the area of the hangar.

3 Copy and complete this table.

	Scale	Scaled length	Actual length
a	1 cm to 2 m		24 m
b	1 cm to 5 km	9.2 cm	
c		6 cm	42 miles
d	5 cm to 8 m	30 cm	

4 This diagram shows a scale drawing of a supermarket.

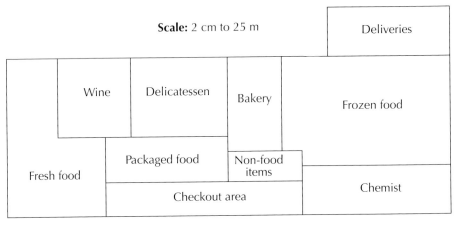

Make a table showing the dimensions and area of each section of the supermarket.

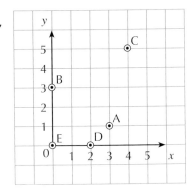

Practice

15C Coordinates in all four quadrants

1 Write down the coordinates of the points A, B, C, D and E.

2 a Make a copy of the grid in Question 1 and plot new points A(1, 1), B(3, 1) and C(5, 4).
  b The three points, A, B and C, are the vertices of a parallelogram. Plot the point D to complete the parallelogram.

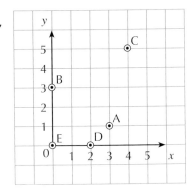

3 Write down the coordinates of the points G, H, I, J, K, L and M.

4 **a** Make a copy of the grid in Question 3 and plot new points G(–5, –3), H(–5, 4) and I(2, 4).
   b Join the points, G, H and I, to make a triangle.
   c Plot point J so that GHIJ is a square. Draw the other two sides of the square.
   d The diagonal, GI, of the square crosses the axes at two points. Write down their coordinates.

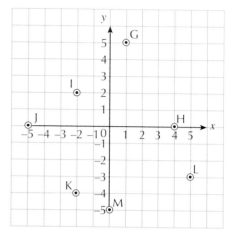

Practice

15D Constructing triangles

1 Construct these triangles. Label your diagrams.

a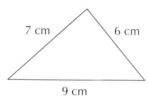

b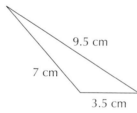

c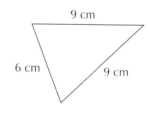

2 Construct each of these triangles.
[**Hint:** Make a rough sketch of the triangle before you draw it accurately.]
   a △ABC where AB = 9 cm, BC = 7 cm and AC = 7 cm
   b △PQR where PQ = 7 cm, QR = 3.5 cm and PR = 9 cm

3 Construct these triangles using ruler, compasses and a protractor.

a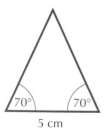

b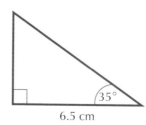

c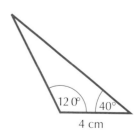

5

1. Use your protractor to find the marked angles. Write down the bearing of B from A. (**Remember:** use three figures.)

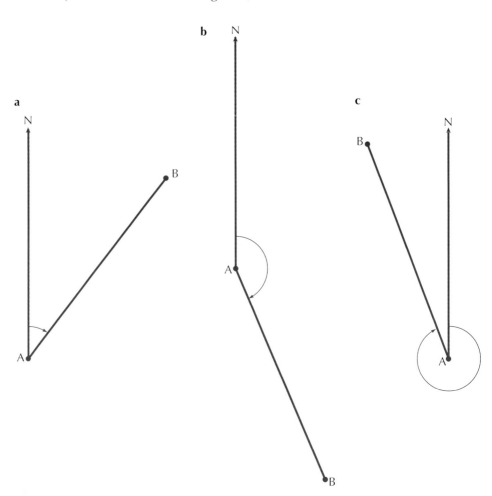

2. Find the bearing of P from Q.

a

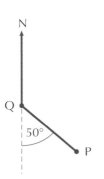

b

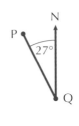

c

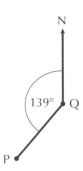

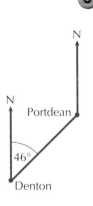
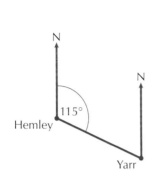
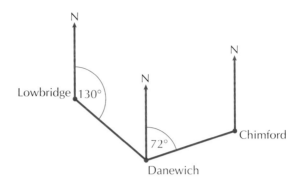

Write down bearing of:
a Portdean from Denton **b** Yarr from Hemley
c Chimford from Danewich **d** Danewich from Lowbridge

 Sketch these bearings. Label your diagrams.

a A skier is on a bearing of 72° from the ski lodge.
b Clerkhill is 12 miles from Moffat on a bearing of 115°.

CHAPTER **16** Statistics **3**

Practice

16A Frequency tables

1 This table shows the lengths of some python snakes, measured to the nearest metre.

Length of snake (m)	Frequency
0 – 1	2
2 – 4	4
5 – 8	7
9 – 11	9

a One of the snakes is 6 m long. Which class contains this length?
b How many snakes are shorter than 5 metres?
c How many snakes have a length of 5 metres or more?
d How many snakes are between 2 and 8 metres long, inclusive?
e How many snakes were measured?
Five more snakes are measured.
Their lengths are 3 m, 8 m, 4 m, 1 m and 10 m.
f Copy and update the table to include these five snakes.

2 These are the durations of 30 telephone calls.

4	12	8	1	19	7	7	28	14	54
9	2	20	16	2	43	5	18	1	5
5	14	9	10	3	30	11	6	17	2

Times have been rounded up to the nearest minute.
Copy and complete this table.

Length of telephone call (minutes)	Tally	Frequency
1 – 10		
11 – 20		
21 – 30		
31 – 40		
41 – 50		
51 – 60		

3 These are the volumes of liquid contained in 20 coconuts, measured in millilitres.

| 12.0 | 11.1 | 10.5 | 12.8 | 12.0 | 10.1 | 11.8 | 12.3 | 10.7 | 12.7 |
| 10.0 | 11.6 | 12.1 | 10.5 | 10.8 | 12.6 | 10.7 | 11.4 | 12.8 | 11.3 |

Copy and complete this frequency table.

Volume of liquid (ml)	Number of coconuts
10.0 – 10.4	
10.5 – 10.9	
11.0 – 11.4	
11.5 – 11.9	
12.0 – 12.4	
12.5 – 12.9	

Practice

16B The median

1 Find the median of these sets of data.
(**Remember:** order the numbers from smallest to largest.)

a 9, 3, 4, 8, 9, 4, 4
b 30, 20, 20, 70, 45, 10, 55, 30, 60, 25, 90
c £28, £83, £19, £44, £20, £71, £43, £16, £99
d 5 m, 7.5 m, 1 m, 3.5 m, 6.5 m

2 Find the median of these sets of data.

a 5, 5, 0, 2, 2, 4
b 23, 21, 19, 21, 21, 21, 18, 25
c 8 kg, 4 kg, 9 kg, 9 kg, 6 kg, 12 kg, 4 kg, 3 kg, 9 kg, 9 kg
d 300 mm, 100 mm, 250 mm, 600 mm, 400 mm, 800 mm

3 **a** Write down a set of three numbers whose median is 4.
   b Write down a set of four numbers whose median is 4.
   c Write down a set of seven numbers whose median is 20.

4 This table shows the points scored by eight robots in school Robot Wars.

Robot	Score
Buzz Chainsaw	78
Cracker	23
Flipper	55
Electro	37
Fireball 2	83
Ram Rod	46
Speedy	71
Pounder	50

   a Calculate the median score.
   b If Ram Rod had scored 50 points, would the median change?

5 Sara found that the median number of children in 10 families was 3.5. How many families had 3 or fewer children?

Practice

16C Constructing frequency diagrams

1 This table shows which method of transport pupils enjoyed the most.

Method of transport	Number of pupils
Roller skates	5
Bicycle	12
Skateboard	9
Scooter	7

Construct a bar chart for the data.

2 This table shows the numbers of goals scored in some football matches.

Number of goals	Number of matches
0	8
1	13
2	20
3	18
4	15
5	7

Construct a bar-line graph for the data.

3 This table shows the times some runners took to complete a 10-km race.

Time taken (minutes)	Number of runners
20 – 39	6
40 – 59	13
60 – 79	24
80 – 99	38
100 – 119	20

Construct a bar chart for the data.

16D Comparing averages and ranges

1 QuickDrive and Ground Works are two companies that lay drives. The numbers of days they take to complete 9 similar drives are shown below.

QuickDrive	2, 5, 3, 3, 6, 2, 1, 8, 3
Ground Works	3, 2, 3, 1, 4, 3, 2, 2, 1

a i Calculate the mode for each company.
 ii Compare the modes.
b i Calculate the median for each company.
 ii Compare the medians.
c i Calculate the range for each company.
 ii Compare the ranges.
d Which company is the most consistent?

2 This table shows the weights of fish three anglers caught in a competition.

Jerry	Aditya	Marion
230 g	230 g	100 g
100 g	400 g	130 g
380 g	280 g	430 g
720 g	320 g	200 g
450 g	250 g	70 g
		180 g
		200 g
		90 g

a i Calculate the range for each of the anglers.
 ii Who was the most consistent? Explain your answer.
b i Calculate the median for each of the anglers.
 ii Who performed the best overall? Explain your answer.
c Which angler would you choose to enter a competition that offered prizes for the heaviest fish caught? Explain your answer.

FM **3** This table shows the mean and range of the weekly rainfall in two holiday resorts.

	Larmidor	Tutu Island
Mean	6.5 mm	5 mm
Range	33 mm	62 mm

Explain the advantages of each island's climate using the mean and range.

Practice

16E Which average to use?

1 The average of each set of data has been given. State why the average given is the best average to use.

a 5, 5, 7, 9, 9, 10, 12   Mean = 8.25
b 3, 4, 4, 5, 5, 7, 100, 200   Median = 5
c 1, 1, 2, 2, 3, 8, 100   Mean = 16.7
d 21, 22, 24, 24, 25   Mode = 24
e 7, 7, 8, 9, 10   Mode = 7
f 0, 1, 1, 2, 20, 20, 21   Median = 2

2 Judges awarded these points to competitors in a surfing competition.

12, 14, 14, 24, 28, 33, 36, 39, 40, 42, 48

a Calculate the mean. Is this a suitable measure of the average?
b Calculate the median. Is this a suitable measure of the average?
c Find the mode. Is this a suitable measure of the average?

3 Two shops offer these sizes of dresses.

Periwinkle	12, 14, 16, 18, 30
Jenny's	10, 12, 14, 16, 18, 20, 22

a Which shop has the greatest range of sizes?
b Do you think the range is a suitable measure? Explain your answer.

Practice

16F Experimental and theoretical probability

1 There are four possible results of flipping two ordinary coins at the same time.

a   What is the theoretical probability of flipping two Heads? Write your answer as a decimal.
b   Flip two coins 20 times and record the results.
c   Calculate the experimental probability of flipping two Heads. Write your answer as a decimal.
d   Compare the experimental and theoretical probabilities. Are they close?
e   How could you obtain a closer experimental probability?

2 Lena arranged these raffle tickets in three rows for people to choose from.

1	2	3	4	5	6	7	8	9	10
11	12	13	14	15	16	17	18	19	20
21	22	23	24	25	26	27	28	29	30

She predicted that people are more likely to choose a number from the middle row than the outer rows.

a   What is the theoretical probability of someone choosing a number from the middle row?
b   Carry out an investigation to test Lena's prediction.

Your Notes

Your Notes